Johnny Morris's Animal Story Book

Johnny Morris, universally known and loved for his television programme *Animal Magic*, presents his own selection of favourite animal stories and poems. This is a collection to delight every animal lover, featuring authors such as James Herriott, Gavin Maxwell, Gerald Durrell and Rudyard Kipling . . . all introduced in Johnny Morris's inimitable style.

Johnny Morris has written several books for children, including *Animal Quiz*, a Beaver book.

JOHNNY MORRIS'S
Animal Story Book

Illustrated by Tony Morris

Beaver Books

First published in 1980 by
The Hamlyn Publishing Group Limited
London · New York · Sydney · Toronto
Astronaut House, Feltham, Middlesex, England
Paperback Division: Hamlyn Paperbacks,
Banda House, Cambridge Grove,
Hammersmith, London W6 0LE
Scholastic edition 1981

© Copyright this collection and
introductory texts Johnny Morris 1980
© Copyright Illustrations The Hamlyn Publishing Group Limited

ISBN 0 600 20396 4

Typeset, printed and bound in Great Britain by
Hazell Watson & Viney Limited, Aylesbury, Bucks
Set in Monotype Garamond

Contents

Acknowledgements

The author and publishers would like to thank the following people for giving permission to include in this anthology material which is their copyright.

Gerald Duckworth & Co Ltd for 'The Big Baboon' from *The Complete Verse of Hilaire Belloc*

Evans Brothers Ltd for 'Zoo Manners' from *Come Follow Me* by Eileen Mathias

Faber and Faber Ltd for 'Cholmondeley the Chimpanzee', an extract from *The Overloaded Ark* by Gerald Durrell; and 'The Rum Tum Tugger' from *Old Possum's Book of Practical Cats* by T. S. Eliot

David Higham Associates Ltd for 'Oscar', an extract from *Vet in a Spin* by James Herriot, published by Michael Joseph; and 'Emma', an extract from *Emma and I* by Sheila Hocken, published by Gollancz

Michael Joseph Ltd for 'Bill Brock', an extract from *A Weasel in My Meatsafe* by Phil Drabble

Macmillan, London and Basingstoke, for 'Bear' and 'Parrot' from *Brownjohn's Beasts* by Alan Brownjohn

Oxford University Press for 'Cows' from *The Blackbird in the Lilac* by James Reeves (1952)

Penguin Books Ltd for 'Mijbil', extracts from *The Otters' Tale* by Gavin Maxwell

Laurence Pollinger Ltd for 'Flicka', an extract from *My Friend Flicka* by Mary O'Hara, published by Eyre Methuen Ltd

The Society of Authors as the literary representative of the Estate of Rose Fyleman for 'Mice'

A. P. Watt Ltd, the National Trust and Macmillan London Ltd for 'The Elephant's Child' from *Just So Stories* by Rudyard Kipling

Introduction

The most compelling thing about an animal is its character. There are dogs and cats that have travelled hundreds of miles on their own, back to a place where they were born or where they have lived. I once had a cat who time after time went back to the house where he was born – he just could not get used to our new house. He met with a fatal road accident on one of his pilgrimages to the old house.

We have all of us at some time known animals with strong characters. Not just cats and dogs, but bantams, pigs, sheep and cows. You have only to watch a herd of cows wandering to the milking parlour: the same few cows always insist that they are the first to be milked. They usually have most aristocratic faces.

The stories and poems I have chosen are about animals with forceful characters and I hope that you will see them as I do, as people. We totally control the animals of this world – we can do just what we like with them. They generally are quite prepared to accept this so the least we can do is to consider them as our equals and respect them.

There was a time, not so very long ago, when there were more horses in Britain than there were people. Those horses worked for us because we trained them to do so. We made them pull ploughs, haul carts, and carry us about. And very good at it they were. You could travel all over the country very cheaply and surprisingly quickly by stage coach. The run from London to Brighton could be done in under four hours. In those days pretty well everybody handled horses or was connected with them in some way, for our very lives depended on them. We knew horses as well as we knew people; and, like people, each horse had its own character.

This one was a glutton for work, this one was lazy. Keep well away from the hindquarters of that one, he kicks. Don't get too near the head of that one, he bites. Some horses were very difficult to catch in the open, some were easy. Some horses were naturally kind and good-tempered, others were irritable and moody. Some were stupid, some were clever, and some would always amble slowly home even if the driver in the cart behind was sound asleep and snoring. The baker's horse, the milkman's horse, the coalman's horse, the greengrocer's horse: they all plodded the city streets moving on their own while the tradesman tapped the doors delivering the goods. They knew just when to stop and when to 'Gee-up'.

We knew them very well and they knew us very well. They adapted to the strangest conditions by using what we called Horse Sense. Horse Sense basically means that if you have done a certain thing once then it will be reasonably safe to do it again. But if you are confronted with something that you have never done before then you are extremely careful about doing it. Some horses had good Horse Sense. Some did not. People, I think, are very much the same, and I'm sure that we learned a good deal from horses. Be careful, don't do anything silly, you might get hurt, find out first of all. Horse Sense. I'm afraid that we have lost a good deal of it now that the horses are gone and we are dependent on the motor car. I know that lots of people give their motor cars names like 'Lizzie' or 'Whizzbang' but this is just an attempt to give something some sort of character that it doesn't really possess.

A few months ago I visited an RSPCA Animal Centre. It was a beautiful summer day and I strolled around the pens that held some very fine-looking dogs and cats. They were all orphans. They were lost, abandoned or put there in the hope that homes would be found for them. It is always a sad sight to see so many animals simply asking for human companionship and affection. I wistfully eyed the dogs and walked over to the cats. I think he was the fifth cat I looked at but he looked at me, smiled and winked. I asked him if he would like to come back to my place. He said he'd give it a go. He is a very clever cat with a lot of character and personality. I forgot to say that he is also extremely beautiful but it was his smile and wink that won me over. He is a tiger tabby with four white paws. His name had to be 'Smarty Boots'. An animal with character will always name itself.

Cholmondeley the Chimpanzee

Gerald Durrell

Shorty before we left our hill-top hut at Bekabe and travelled down to our last camp at Kumba, we had to stay with us a most unusual guest in the shape of Cholmondeley, known to his friends as Chumley.

Chumley was a full-grown chimpanzee; his owner, a District Officer, was finding the ape's large size rather awkward, and he wanted to send him to London Zoo as a present, so that he could visit the animal when he was back in England on leave. He wrote asking us if we would mind taking Chumley back with us when we left, and depositing him at his new home in London, and we replied that we would not mind at all. I don't think that either John or myself had the least idea how big Chumley was: I know that I visualised an ape of about three years old, standing about three feet high. I got a rude shock when Chumley moved in.

He arrived in the back of a small van, seated sedately in a huge crate. When the doors of his crate were opened and Chumley stepped out with all the ease and self-confidence of a film star, I was considerably shaken for, standing on his bow legs in a normal slouching chimp position, he came up to my waist, and if he had straightened up, his head would have been on a level with my chest. He had huge arms, and must have measured at least twice my measurements round his hairy chest. Owing to bad tooth growth both sides of his face were swollen out of all proportion, and this gave him a weird pugilistic look. His eyes were small, deep set and intelligent; the top of his head was nearly bald owing, I discovered later, to his habit of sitting and rubbing the palms of his hands backwards across his head, an exercise which seemed to afford him much pleasure and which he persisted in until the top of his skull was quite devoid of hair. This was no young chimp, as I had expected, but a veteran of about eight or nine years old, fully mature, strong as a powerful man and, to judge by his expression, with considerable experience of life. Although he was not exactly a nice chimp to look at (I had seen more handsome), he certainly had a terrific personality: it hit you as soon as you set eyes on him. His little eyes looked at you with a great intelligence, and there seemed to be a glitter of ironic laughter in their depths that made one feel uncomfortable.

He stood on the ground and surveyed his surroundings with a shrewd glance, and then he turned to me and held out one of his soft, pink-palmed hands to be shaken, with exactly that bored expression that one sees on the faces of professional hand-shakers. Round his neck was a thick chain, and its length dropped over the tailboard of the lorry and disappeared into the depths of his crate. With an animal of less personality than Chumley, this would have been a sign of his subjugation, of his captivity. But Chumley wore the chain with the superb air of a Lord Mayor; after shaking my hand so professionally, he turned and proceeded to pull the chain, which measured some fifteen feet, out of his crate. He gathered it up carefully into loops, hung it over one hand and proceeded to walk into the hut as if he owned it. Thus, in the first few minutes of arrival, Chumley had made us feel inferior, and had moved in not, we felt, because we wanted it, but because he did. I almost felt I ought to apologise for the mess on the table when he walked in.

He seated himself in a chair, dropped his chain on the floor, and then looked hopefully at me. It was quite obvious that he expected some sort of refreshment after his tiring journey. I roared out to the kitchen for them to make a cup of tea, for I had been warned that Chumley had a great liking for the cup that cheers. Leaving him sitting in the chair and surveying our humble abode with ill-concealed disgust, I went out to his crate, and in it I found a tin plate and a battered tin mug of colossal proportions. When I returned to the hut bearing these Chumley brightened considerably, and even went so far as to praise me for my intelligence.

'Ooooooo, umph!' he said, and then crossed his legs and continued his inspection of the hut. I sat down opposite him and produced a packet of cigarettes. As I was selecting one a long black arm was stretched across the table, and Chumley grunted in delight. Wondering what he would do I handed him a cigarette, and to my astonishment he put it carefully in the corner of his mouth. I lit my smoke and handed Chumley the matches thinking that this would fool him. He opened the box, took out a match, struck it, lit his cigarette, threw the matches down on the table, crossed his legs again and lay back in his chair inhaling thankfully, and

blowing clouds of smoke out of his nose. Obviously he had vices in his make-up of which I had been kept in ignorance.

Just at that moment Pious entered bearing the tray of tea: the effect on him when he saw me sitting at the table with the chimp, smoking and apparently exchanging gossip, was considerable.

'Eh . . . eahh!' he gasped, backing away.

'Whar . . . hooo,' said Chumley, sighting the tea and waving one hand madly.

'Na whatee that, sah?' asked Pious from the doorway.

'This is Chumley,' I explained, 'he won't hurt you. Put the tea on the table.'

Pious did as he was told and then retreated to the door again. As I poured tea and milk into Chumley's mug, and added three tablespoons of sugar, he watched me with a glittering eye, and made a soft 'ooing' noise to himself. I handed him the mug and he took it carefully in both hands. There was a moment's confusion when he tried to rid himself of the cigarette, which he found he could not hold as well as the mug; he solved the problem by placing the cigarette on the table. Then he tested the tea carefully with one lip stuck out, to see if it was too hot. As it was, he sat there and blew on it until it was the right temperature, and then he drank it down. When he had finished the liquid there still remained the residue of syrupy sugar at the bottom, and as Chumley's motto was obviously waste not want not, he balanced the mug on his nose and kept it there until the last of the sugar had trickled down into his mouth. Then he held it out for a refill.

Chumley's crate was placed at a convenient point about fifty yards from the hut, next to a great gnarled tree stump to which I attached his chain. From here he could get a good view of everything that went on in and around the hut, and as we were working he would shout comments to me and I would reply. That first day he created an uproar, for no sooner had I left him chained up and gone into the hut to do some work, than a frightful upheaval took place among the monkeys. All these were tethered on ropes under a palm leaf shelter just opposite the hut. Chumley, after I had left him, felt bored, so looking around he perceived some sizeable rocks lying about within easy reach. Arming himself with these he proceeded to have a little underarm bowling practice. The first I knew of this was when I heard shrill screams and chatterings from the Drills and Guenons, and dashing out I was just in time to see a rock the size of a cabbage land in their midst, fortunately missing them all. If one of these rocks had hit a monkey it would have been squashed flat. Seizing a stick I raced down upon Chumley waving it and shouting at him, trying to appear fearsome, while all the time I was wondering what was going to happen if I tried to deal out punishment to an animal almost my own size and with twice my strength, when I was armed with only a short stick that seemed ridiculously flimsy. However, to my surprise, Chumley saw me coming and promptly lay on the ground, covering his face and his head with his long arms, and proceeded to scream at the top of his voice. I gave him two cuts with the stick across his back, and it had about as much effect as if I had tried to demolish St Paul's

Cathedral with a toothpick. His back was broad and flat, solid muscle as hard as iron.

'You are a very wicked animal,' I said sternly, and Chumley, realising that punishment was apparently over, sat up and started to remove bits of leaf from himself.

'Whooooooo . . .' he said, glancing up at me shyly.

'If you do that again I will have to give you a really good beating,' I continued, wondering if anything short of a tree trunk would make any impression on him.

'Arrrrr . . . ooo,' said Chumley. He shifted forward, squatted down and commenced to roll up my trouser leg, and then search my calf for any spots, bits of dirt, or other microscopic blemishes. While he was thus engaged I called the animal staff and had them remove every rock from the vicinity. Later, after giving the beast yet another talking to, I left him, and shortly afterwards I noticed him digging hopefully in the earth near his crate, presumably in search of more rocks.

That night, when I carried Chumley's food and drink of tea out to him, he greeted me with loud 'hoo hoos' of delight, and jogged up and down beating his knuckles on the ground. Before he touched his dinner, however, he seized one of my hands in his and carried it to his mouth. With some trepidation I watched as he carefully put one of my fingers between his great teeth and very gently bit it. Then I understood: in the chimpanzee world to place your finger between another ape's teeth and do the same with his, is a greeting and sign of trust, for to place a finger in such a vulnerable position is a sure display of your belief in the other's friendliness. So Chumley was flattering me by treating me as he would another chimp. Then he set to and soon polished off his meal. When he had finished I sat beside him on the ground, and he went carefully through my pockets and examined everything I had on me.

When I decided that it was time he went to bed he refused to give back a handkerchief which he had removed. He held it behind his back and passed it from one hand to the other as I tried to get it. Then, thinking that the action would settle the matter, he stuffed it hurriedly into his mouth. I realised that if I gave in and let him keep the handkerchief he would think that he could get away with anything, so for half an hour I sat there pleading and cajoling with him, until eventually, very reluctantly, he disgorged it, now very sodden and crumpled. After this I had no trouble with him: if he was playing with something that I wanted I would simply hold out my hand and ask him for it, and he would give it to me without any fuss.

Now, I had known a great number of attractive and charming animals from mice to elephants, but I have never seen one to compare with Chumley for force and charm of personality, or for intelligence. After knowing him for a while you ceased to look upon him as an animal; you regarded him more as a wizard, a mischievous, courtly old man, who had, for some reason best known to himself, disguised himself as a chimpanzee.

From *The Overloaded Ark*

I don't think we fully realise what wonderful animals cows are. Many people call them stupid and thick-headed and I can understand this feeling. When you happen to be driving along a country lane and you come up behind a herd of cows being driven along to be milked – oh! they are so slow, and they don't seem to care two hoots whether you are in a hurry or not. They even stop and crop a lush tuffet of grass growing on top of the ditch. They are enough to try the patience of a saint. But just think of what they do for us. They give us for free all that milk, to be made into all that butter. They never complain. They allow us to milk and milk them year after year. They give it all to us for nothing. Perhaps that is why some people call them stupid. But cows are like that. So generous, so placid, so ready to be told what to do.

When I worked on a farm we often had to get the cows into a small yard to treat them for certain trouble-some parasites. I frequently had to push my way through this great mass of cows, and I never ceased to be impressed by the way they stood quietly and calmly and just waited. There must have been about 30 tonnes of solid cow in that yard. They could have crushed me to a pulp had they wanted to, but they never did because they trusted the people that handled them, fed them and milked them. In other words we had won their confidence. And this applies to all animals with which we share our lives. We must gain their confidence. We must persuade them to trust us. Once we have done that the rest is fairly simple. It is easier for some people than it is for others. I'll try to explain.

On our farm we had five separate herds of milking cows. There was a cowman in charge of each herd. Each cowman had a different personality. Harry was slow and never lost his temper. Harry's cows were slow and never got in a panic. Charlie was brisk and businesslike. Charlie's cows seemed to move just that bit quicker and went into their stalls very neatly. George was a very nice man but he sometimes used to yell and shout at his cows. George's cows were very nice cows but they were a bit nervous and jumpy because they never knew when they were going to be shouted at. They say that people grow like their animals. Perhaps so. But of this I am certain, animals do take on the characters of their owners. The next poem is about cows. Two very untroubled cows who must have had an owner with few worries of his own, and who certainly never worried them.

Cows

James Reeves

Half the time they munched the grass,
   and all the time they lay
Down in the water-meadows, the lazy month
   of May,
      A-chewing,
      A-mooing,
   To pass the time away.
   Nice weather,
                  said the brown cow.
Ah,
      said the white.
   Grass is very tasty.
   Grass is all right.

Half the time they munched the grass,
   and all the time they lay
Down in the water-meadows, the lazy month
   of May,
      A-chewing,
      A-mooing,
   To pass the time away.
   Rain coming,
                  said the brown cow.

Ah,
    said the white.
Flies is very tiresome.
Flies bite.

Half the time they munched the grass,
  and all the time they lay
Down in the water-meadows, the lazy month
  of May,
    A-chewing,
    A-mooing,
  To pass the time away.
  Time to go,
          said the brown cow.
Ah,
    said the white.
Nice chat.
Very pleasant.
Night.
Night.

Half the time they munched the grass,
  and half the time they lay
Down in the water-meadows, the lazy month
  of May,
    A-chewing,
    A-mooing,
  To pass the time away.

From *The Blackbird in the Lilac*

As a country vet James Herriot was much used to dealing with cows and other farm animals, although he had to look after pets as well. It takes a lot of study and a lot of training to be a vet, and even when you qualify there is still much to learn through hard experience. When you work on a farm, too, you have to learn by experience how to give first aid to animals. Some of the remedies we applied would no doubt shock the modern vet but some of them seemed to work.

I'll never forget when I was quite a young lad seeing a cow that had knocked her horn off. This happened now and again: two cows would have a disagreement about something or other and start to fight. They put their heads down, locked horns and started shoving and pushing. In an open field this was not too bad – it was only a token fight in any case to show who was the boss. But if the tussle happened in a yard or near some buildings the tusslers could bang into a wall and then one could get her horn knocked off.

You have probably seen a cow's hollow horn. Well, when it's on the cow it covers a hard bony substance, and when the horn gets knocked off the protrusion that's left just bleeds and bleeds and bleeds. It is a quite horrific sight to see a cow with blood gushing down its face.

I remember I said to the cowman, 'Oh gosh, I'd better get the vet.' He just gave me a strange sideways look to make sure I wasn't frothing at the mouth or something. 'What d'you want to get a vet for?' 'Well, she looks as though she'll bleed to death.' 'Look, help I get 'er in the shed.'

We steered her into a shed, a trail of blood splattering behind her. One part of the shed was used to store cattle cake. It hung heavy with cobwebs: not the round cartwheel sort of cobwebs, but cobwebs that sagged like hammocks, and had been slung up there for years. They were weighed down with dust that had drifted up from the bags of cattle cake.

The poor old cow just stood looking mournfully at the cowman. She knew him well and watched him as he climbed up on the bags of cattle cake. The cow and I watched him. What was he doing? He reached up towards the cobwebs. His hands were big, bony and blotched. But he somehow, very delicately, unhitched a great big droop of cobweb and, holding it very carefully with hands wide apart, he jumped down from the bags of cattle cake. 'Just hold 'er a minute.'

I held the cow by her good horn with one hand and by the nose with the other. The cowman, holding the heavy cobweb, paused for a second or so and then, almost like a ballet dancer waving a scarf, he slung the cobweb around the bleeding stump of horn. It was a most graceful movement, and there stood the cow wearing a gossamer bandage on her painful stump. The bleeding stopped almost at once. The spiders had spun a bandage far finer than we could have done.

We washed the cow's face free of blood and turned her out into the field with the other cows. She started grazing straight away and then just turned her sad face to the gateway where the cowman and I were standing. She stared at us for a second or so and then went on cropping the grass. Perhaps she said quietly when she gazed at us, 'Very kind of you, I'm sure, thanks.'

Oscar

James Herriot

'Jim! Jim!'

I went out and stuck my head over the banisters. 'What is it, Triss?'

'Sorry to bother you, Jim, but could you come down for a minute?' The upturned face had an anxious look.

I went down the long flights of steps two at a time and when I arrived slightly breathless on the ground floor Tristan beckoned me through to the consulting room at the back of the house. A teenage girl was standing by the table, her hand resting on a stained roll of blanket.

'It's a cat,' Tristan said. He pulled back a fold of the blanket and I looked down at a large, deeply striped tabby. At least he would have been large if he had had any flesh on his bones, but ribs and pelvis stood out painfully through the fur and as I passed my hand over the motionless body I could feel only a thin covering of skin.

Tristan cleared his throat. 'There's something else, Jim.'

I looked at him curiously. For once he didn't seem to have a joke in him. I watched as he gently lifted one of the cat's hind legs and rolled the abdomen into view. There was a gash on the ventral surface through which a coiled cluster of intestines spilled grotesquely on to the cloth. I was still shocked and staring when the girl spoke.

'I saw this cat sittin' in the dark, down Brown's yard. I thought 'e looked skinny, like, and a bit quiet and I bent down to give 'im a pat. Then I saw 'e was badly hurt and I went home for a blanket and brought 'im round to you.'

'That was kind of you,' I said. 'Have you any idea who he belongs to?'

The girl shook her head. 'No, he looks like a stray to me.'

'He does indeed.' I dragged my eyes away from the terrible wound. 'You're Marjorie Simpson, aren't you?'

'Yes.'

'I know your Dad well. He's our postman.'

'That's right.' She gave a half smile then her lips trembled. 'Well, I reckon I'd better leave 'im with you. You'll be goin' to put him out of his misery. There's nothing anybody can do about . . . about that?'

I shrugged and shook my head. The girl's eyes filled with tears, she stretched out a hand and touched the emaciated animal then turned and walked quickly to the door.

'Thanks again, Marjorie,' I called after the retreating back. 'And don't worry – we'll look after him.'

In the silence that followed, Tristan and I looked down at the shattered animal. Under the surgery lamp it was all too easy to see. He had almost been disembowelled and the pile of intestines was covered in dirt and mud.

'What d'you think did this?' Tristan said at length. 'Has he been run over?'

'Maybe,' I replied. 'Could be anything. An attack by a big dog or somebody could have kicked him or struck him.' All things were possible with cats because some people seemed to regard them as fair game for any cruelty.

Tristan nodded. 'Anyway, whatever happened, he must have been on the verge of starvation. He's a skeleton. I bet he's wandered miles from home.'

'Ah well,' I sighed. 'There's only one thing to do. Those guts are perforated in several places. It's hopeless.'

Tristan didn't say anything but he whistled under his breath and drew the tip of his forefinger again and again across the furry cheek. And, unbelievably, from somewhere in the scraggy chest a gentle purring arose.

The young man looked at me, round-eyed. 'My God, do you hear that?'

'Yes . . . amazing in that condition. He's a good-natured cat.'

Tristan, head bowed, continued his stroking. I knew how he felt because, although he preserved a cheerfully hard-boiled attitude to our patients he couldn't kid me about one thing; he had a soft spot for cats. Even now, when we are both around the sixty mark, he often talks to me over a beer about the cat he has had for many years. It is a typical relationship – they tease each other unmercifully – but it is based on real affection.

'It's no good, Triss,' I said gently. 'It's got to be done.' I reached for the syringe but something in me rebelled against plunging a needle into that mutilated body. Instead I pulled a fold of the blanket over the cat's head.

'Pour a little ether on to the cloth,' I said. 'He'll just sleep away.'

Wordlessly Tristan unscrewed the cap of the ether bottle and poised it above the head. Then from under the shapeless heap of blanket we heard it again; the deep purring which increased in volume till it boomed in our ears like a distant motorcycle.

Tristan was like a man turned to stone, hand gripping the bottle rigidly, eyes staring down at the mound of cloth from which the purring rose in waves of warm friendly sound.

At last he looked up at me and gulped. 'I don't fancy this much, Jim. Can't we do something?'

'You mean, put that lot back?'

'Yes.'

'But the bowels are damaged – they're like a sieve in parts.'

'We could stitch them, couldn't we?'

I lifted the blanket and looked again. 'Honestly, Triss, I wouldn't know where to start. And the whole thing is filthy.'

He didn't say anything, but continued to look at me steadily. And I didn't need much persuading. I had no more desire to pour ether on to that comradely purring than he had.

'Come on, then,' I said. 'We'll have a go.'

With the oxygen bubbling and the cat's head in the anaesthetic mask we washed the whole prolapse with warm saline. We did it again and again but it was impossible to remove every fragment of caked dirt. Then we started the painfully slow business of stitching the many holes in the tiny intestines, and here I was glad of Tristan's nimble fingers which seemed better able to manipulate the small round-bodied needles than mine.

Two hours and yards of catgut later, we dusted the patched up peritoneal surface with sulphonamide and pushed the entire mass back into the abdomen. When I had sutured muscle layers and skin everything looked tidy but I had a nasty feeling of sweeping undesirable things under the carpet. The extensive damage, all that contamination – peritonitis was inevitable.

'He's alive, anyway, Triss,' I said as we began to wash the instruments. 'We'll put him on to sulpha-pyridine and keep our fingers crossed.' There were still no antibiotics at that time but the new drug was a big advance.

The door opened and Helen came in. 'You've been a long time, Jim.' She walked over to the table and looked down at the sleeping cat. 'What a poor skinny little thing. He's all bones.'

'You should have seen him when he came in.' Tristan switched off the steriliser and screwed shut the valve on the anaesthetic machine. 'He looks a lot better now.'

She stroked the little animal for a moment. 'Is he badly injured?'

'I'm afraid so, Helen,' I said. 'We've done our best for him but I honestly don't think he has much chance.'

'What a shame. And he's pretty, too. Four white feet and all those unusual colours.' With her finger she traced the faint bands of auburn and copper-gold among the grey and black.

Tristan laughed. 'Yes, I think that chap has a ginger tom somewhere in his ancestry.'

Helen smiled, too, but absently, and I noticed a

broody look about her. She hurried out to the stock room and returned with an empty box.

'Yes . . . yes . . .' she said thoughtfully. 'I can make a bed in this box for him and he'll sleep in our room, Jim.'

'He will?'

'Yes, he must be warm, mustn't he?'

'Of course.'

Later, in the darkness of our bed-sitter, I looked from my pillow at a cosy scene; Sam in his basket on one side of the flickering fire and the cat cushioned and blanketed in his box on the other.

As I floated off into sleep it was good to know that my patient was so comfortable, but I wondered if he would be alive in the morning . . .

I knew he was alive at 7.30 a.m. because my wife was already up and talking to him. I trailed across the room in my pyjamas and the cat and I looked at each other. I rubbed him under the chin and he opened his mouth in a rusty miaow. But he didn't try to move.

'Helen,' I said. 'This little thing is tied together inside with catgut. He'll have to live on fluids for a week and even then he probably won't make it. If he stays up here you'll be spooning milk into him umpteen times a day.'

'Okay, okay.' She had that broody look again.

It wasn't only milk she spooned into him over the next few days. Beef essence, strained broth and a succession of sophisticated baby foods found their way down his throat at regular intervals. One lunch time I found Helen kneeling by the box.

'We shall call him Oscar,' she said.

'You mean we're keeping him?'

'Yes.'

I am fond of cats but we already had a dog in our cramped quarters and I could see difficulties. Still I decided to let it go.

'Why Oscar?'

'I don't know.' Helen tipped a few drops of chop gravy on to the little red tongue and watched intently as he swallowed.

One of the things I like about women is their mystery, the unfathomable part of them, and I didn't press the matter further. But I was pleased at the way things were going. I had been giving the sulphapyridine every six hours and taking the temperature night and morning, expecting all the time to encounter the roaring fever, the vomiting and the tense abdomen of peritonitis. But it never happened.

It was as though Oscar's animal instinct told him he had to move as little as possible because he lay absolutely still day after day and looked up at us – and purred.

His purr became part of our lives and when he eventually left his bed, sauntered through to our kitchen and began to sample Sam's dinner of meat and biscuit it was a moment of triumph. And I didn't spoil it by wondering if he was ready for solid food; I felt he knew.

From then on it was sheer joy to watch the furry scarecrow fill out and grow strong, and as he ate and ate and the flesh spread over his bones the true beauty of his coat showed in the glossy medley of auburn, black and gold. We had a handsome cat on our hands.

Once Oscar had recovered, Tristan was a regular visitor. He probably felt, and rightly, that he, more than I, had saved Oscar's life in the first place and he used to play with him for long periods. His favourite ploy was to push his leg round the corner of the table and withdraw it repeatedly just as the cat pawed at it.

Oscar was justifiably irritated by this teasing but showed his character by lying in wait for Tristan one night and biting him smartly in the ankle before he could start his tricks.

From my own point of view Oscar added many things to our *ménage*. Sam was delighted with him and the two soon became firm friends. Helen adored him and each evening I thought afresh that a nice cat washing his face by the hearth gave extra comfort to a room.

Oscar had been established as one of the family for several weeks when I came in from a late call to find Helen waiting for me with a stricken face.

'What's happened?' I asked.

'It's Oscar – he's gone!'

'Gone? What do you mean?'

'Oh, Jim, I think he's run away.'

I stared at her. 'He wouldn't do that. He often goes down to the garden at night. Are you sure he isn't there?'

'Absolutely. I've searched right into the yard. I've even had a walk round the town. And remember,' her chin quivered, 'he ... he ran away from somewhere before.'

I looked at my watch. 'Ten o'clock. Yes, that is strange. He shouldn't be out at this time.'

As I spoke the front door bell jangled. I galloped down the stairs and as I rounded the corner in the passage I could see Mrs Heslington, the vicar's wife, through the glass. I threw open the door. She was holding Oscar in her arms.

'I believe this is your cat, Mr Herriot,' she said.

'It is indeed, Mrs Heslington. Where did you find him?'

She smiled. 'Well it was rather odd. We were having a meeting of the Mothers' Union at the church house and we noticed the cat sitting there in the room.'

'Just sitting . . . ?'

'Yes, as though he were listening to what we were saying and enjoying it all. It was unusual. When the meeting ended I thought I'd better bring him along to you.'

'I'm most grateful, Mrs Heslington.' I snatched Oscar and tucked him under my arm. 'My wife is distraught – she thought he was lost.'

It was a little mystery. Why should he suddenly take off like that? But since he showed no change in his manner over the ensuing week we put it out of our minds.

Then one evening a man brought in a dog for a distemper inoculation and left the front door open. When I went up to our flat I found that Oscar had disappeared again. This time Helen and I scoured the market-place and side alleys in vain and when we returned at half past nine we were both despondent. It was nearly eleven and we were thinking of bed when the door bell rang.

It was Oscar again, this time resting on the ample stomach of Jack Newbould. Jack was leaning against a doorpost and the fresh country air drifting in from the dark street was richly intermingled with beer fumes.

Jack was a gardener at one of the big houses. He hiccupped gently and gave me a huge benevolent smile. 'Brought your cat, Mr Herriot.'

'Gosh, thanks, Jack!' I said, scooping up Oscar gratefully. 'Where the devil did you find him?'

'Well, s'matter o' fact, 'e sort of found me.'

'What do you mean?'

Jack closed his eyes for a few moments before articulating carefully. 'Thish is a big night, tha knows, Mr Herriot. Darts championship. Lots of t'lads round at t'Dog and Gun – lotsh and lotsh of 'em. Big gatherin'.'

'And our cat was there?'

'Aye, he were there, all right. Sittin' among t'lads. Shpent t'whole evenin' with us.'

'Just sat there, eh?'

'That 'e did.' Jack giggled reminiscently. 'By gaw 'e enjoyed isself. Ah gave 'im a drop o' best bitter out of me own glass and once or twice ah thought 'e was goin' to have a go at chuckin' a dart. He's some cat.' He laughed again.

As I bore Oscar upstairs I was deep in thought. What was going on here? These sudden desertions were upsetting Helen and I felt they could get on my nerves in time.

I didn't have long to wait till the next one. Three nights later he was missing again. This time Helen and I didn't bother to search – we just waited.

He was back earlier than usual. I heard the door bell at nine o'clock. It was the elderly Miss Simpson peering through the glass. And she wasn't holding Oscar – he was prowling on the mat waiting to come in.

Miss Simpson watched with interest as the cat stalked inside and made for the stairs. 'Ah, good, I'm so glad he's come home safely. I knew he was your cat and I've been intrigued by his behaviour all evening.'

'Where . . . may I ask?'

'Oh, at the Women's Institute. He came in shortly after we started and stayed till the end.'

'Really? What exactly was your programme, Miss Simpson?'

'Well, there was a bit of committee stuff, then a short talk with lantern slides by Mr Walters from the water company and we finished with a cake-making competition.'

'Yes . . . yes . . . and what did Oscar do?'

She laughed. 'Mixed with the company, apparently enjoyed the slides and showed great interest in the cakes.'

'I see. And you didn't bring him home?'

'No, he made his own way here. As you know, I have to pass your house and I merely rang your bell to make sure you knew he had arrived.'

'I'm obliged to you, Miss Simpson. We were a little worried.'

I mounted the stairs in record time. Helen was sitting with the cat on her knee and she looked up as I burst in.

'I know about Oscar now,' I said.

'Know what?'

'Why he goes on these nightly outings. He's not running away – he's visiting.'

'Visiting?'

'Yes,' I said. 'Don't you see? He likes getting around, he loves people, especially in groups, and he's interested in what they do. He's a natural mixer.'

35

Helen looked down at the attractive mound of fur curled on her lap. 'Of course . . . that's it . . . he's a socialite!'

'Exactly, a high-stepper!'

'A cat-about-town!'

It all afforded us some innocent laughter and Oscar sat up and looked at us with evident pleasure, adding his own throbbing purr to the merriment. But for Helen and me there was a lot of relief behind it; ever since our cat had started his excursions there had been the gnawing fear that we would lose him, and now we felt secure.

From that night our delight in him increased. There was endless joy in watching this facet of his character unfolding. He did the social round meticulously, taking in most of the activities of the town. He became a familiar figure at whist drives, jumble sales, school concerts and Scout bazaars. Most of the time he was made welcome, but was twice ejected from meetings of the Rural District Council, who did not seem to relish the idea of a cat sitting in on their deliberations.

At first I was apprehensive about his making his way through the streets but I watched him once or twice and saw that he looked both ways before tripping daintily across. Clearly he had excellent traffic sense and this made me feel that his original injury had not been caused by a car.

Taking it all in all, Helen and I felt that it was a kind stroke of fortune which had brought Oscar to us. He was a warm and cherished part of our home life. He added to our happiness.

When the blow fell it was totally unexpected.

I was finishing the evening surgery. I looked round

the door and saw only a man and two little boys.

'Next, please,' I said.

The man stood up. He had no animal with him. He was middle-aged, with the rough weathered face of a farm worker. He twirled a cloth cap nervously in his hands.

'Mr Herriot?' he said.

'Yes, what can I do for you?'

He swallowed and looked me straight in the eyes. 'Ah think you've got ma cat.'

'What?'

'Ah lost ma cat a bit since.' He cleared his throat. 'We used to live at Missdon but ah got a job as plough-man to Mr Horne of Wederly. It was after we moved to Wederly that t'cat went missin'. Ah reckon he was tryin' to find 'is way back to his old home.'

'Wederly? That's on the other side of Brawton – over thirty miles away.'

'Aye, ah knaw, but cats is funny things.'

'But what makes you think I've got him?'

He twisted the cap around a bit more. 'There's a cousin o' mine lives in Darrowby and ah heard tell from 'im about this cat that goes around to meetin's. I 'ad to come. We've been huntin' everywhere.'

'Tell me,' I said. 'This cat you lost. What did he look like?'

'Grey and black and sort o' gingery. Right bonny 'e was. And 'e was allus goin' out to gatherin's.'

A cold hand clutched at my heart. 'You'd better come upstairs. Bring the boys with you.'

Helen was putting some coal on the fire of the bed-sitter.

'Helen,' I said. 'This is Mr – er – I'm sorry, I don't know your name.'

'Gibbons, Sep Gibbons. They called me Septimus because ah was the seventh in family and it looks like ah'm goin' t'same way 'cause we've got six already. These are our two youngest.' The two boys, obvious twins of about eight, looked up at us solemnly.

I wished my heart would stop hammering. 'Mr Gibbons thinks Oscar is his. He lost his cat some time ago.'

My wife put down her little shovel. 'Oh . . . oh . . . I see.' She stood very still for a moment then smiled faintly. 'Do sit down. Oscar's in the kitchen. I'll bring him through.'

She went out and reappeared with the cat in her arms. She hadn't got through the door before the little boys gave tongue.

'Tiger!' they cried. 'Oh, Tiger, Tiger!'

The man's face seemed lit from within. He walked quickly across the floor and ran his big work-roughened hand along the fur.

'Hullo, awd lad,' he said, and turned to me with a radiant smile. 'It's 'im, Mr Herriot. It's 'im awright, and don't 'e look well!'

'You call him Tiger, eh?' I said.

'Aye,' he replied happily. 'It's them gingery stripes. The kids called 'im that. They were broken-hearted when we lost 'im.'

As the two little boys rolled on the floor our Oscar rolled with them, pawing playfully, purring with delight.

Sep Gibbons sat down again. 'That's the way 'e allus went on wi' the family. They used to play with 'im for hours. By gaw we did miss 'im. He were a right favourite.'

I looked at the broken nails on the edge of the cap, at the decent, honest, uncomplicated Yorkshire face so like the many I had grown to like and respect. Farm men like him got thirty shillings a week in those days and it was reflected in the threadbare jacket, the cracked, shiny boots and the obvious hand-me-downs of the boys.

But all three were scrubbed and tidy, the man's face like a red beacon, the children's knees gleaming and their hair carefully slicked across their foreheads. They looked like nice people to me. I didn't know what to say.

Helen said it for me. 'Well, Mr Gibbons.' Her tone had an unnatural brightness. 'You'd better take him.'

The man hesitated. 'Now then, are ye sure, Missis Herriot?'

'Yes . . . yes, I'm sure. He was your cat first.'

'Aye, but some folks 'ud say finders keepers or summat like that. Ah didn't come 'ere to demand 'im back or owt of t'sort.'

'I know you didn't, Mr Gibbons, but you've had him all those years and you've searched for him so hard. We couldn't possibly keep him from you.'

He nodded quickly. 'Well, that's right good of ye.' He paused for a moment, his face serious, then he stooped and picked Oscar up. 'We'll have to be off if we're goin' to catch the eight o'clock bus.'

Helen reached forward, cupped the cat's head in her hands and looked at him steadily for a few seconds. Then she patted the boys' heads. 'You'll take good care of him, won't you?'

'Aye, missis, thank ye, we will that.' The two small faces looked up at her and smiled.

'I'll see you down the stairs, Mr Gibbons,' I said.

On the descent I tickled the furry cheek resting on the man's shoulder and heard for the last time the rich purring. On the front door step we shook hands and they set off down the street. As they rounded the corner of Trengate they stopped and waved, and I waved back at the man, the two children and the cat's head looking back at me over the shoulder.

It was my habit at that time in my life to mount the stairs two or three at a time but on this occasion I trailed upwards like an old man, slightly breathless, throat tight, eyes prickling.

I cursed myself for a sentimental fool but as I reached our door I found a flash of consolation. Helen had taken it remarkably well. She had nursed that cat and grown deeply attached to him, and I'd have thought an unforeseen calamity like this would have upset her terribly. But no, she had behaved calmly and rationally. You never knew with women, but I was thankful.

It was up to me to do as well. I adjusted my features into the semblance of a cheerful smile and marched into the room.

Helen had pulled a chair close to the table and was slumped face down against the wood. One arm cradled her head while the other was stretched in front of her as her body shook with an utterly abandoned weeping.

I had never seen her like this and I was appalled. I tried to say something comforting but nothing stemmed the flow of racking sobs.

Feeling helpless and inadequate I could only sit close

to her and stroke the back of her head. Maybe I could have said something if I hadn't felt just about as bad myself.

You get over these things in time. After all, we told ourselves, it wasn't as though Oscar had died or got lost again – he had gone to a good family who would look after him. In fact he had really gone home.

And of course, we still had our much-loved Sam, although he didn't help in the early stages by sniffing disconsolately where Oscar's bed used to lie, then collapsing on the rug with a long lugubrious sigh.

There was one other thing, too. I had a little notion forming in my mind, an idea which I would spring on Helen when the time was right. It was about a month after that shattering night and we were coming out of the cinema at Brawton at the end of our half day. I looked at my watch.

'Only eight o'clock,' I said. 'How about going to see Oscar?'

Helen looked at me in surprise. 'You mean – drive on to Wederly?'

'Yes, it's only about five miles.'

A smile crept slowly across her face. 'That would be lovely. But do you think they would mind?'

'The Gibbons? No, I'm sure they wouldn't. Let's go.'

Wederly was a big village and the ploughman's cottage was at the far end a few yards beyond the Methodist chapel. I pushed open the garden gate and we walked down the path.

A busy-looking little woman answered my knock. She was drying her hands on a striped towel.

'Mrs Gibbons?' I said.

'Aye, that's me.'

'I'm James Herriot – and this is my wife.'

Her eyes widened uncomprehendingly. Clearly the name meant nothing to her.

'We had your cat for a while,' I added.

Suddenly she grinned and waved her towel at us. 'Oh aye, ah remember now. Sep told me about you. Come in, come in!'

The big kitchen-living room was a tableau of life with six children and thirty shillings a week. Battered furniture, rows of much-mended washing on a pulley, black cooking range and a general air of chaos.

Sep got up from his place by the fire, put down his newspaper, took off a pair of steel-rimmed spectacles and shook hands.

He waved Helen to a sagging armchair. 'Well, it's right nice to see you. Ah've often spoke of ye to t'missis.'

His wife hung up her towel. 'Yes, and I'm glad to meet ye both. I'll get some tea in a minnit.'

She laughed and dragged a bucket of muddy water into a corner. 'I've been washin' football jerseys. Them lads just handed them to me tonight – as if I haven't enough to do.'

As she ran the water into the kettle I peeped surreptitiously around me and I noticed Helen doing the same. But we searched in vain. There was no sign of a cat. Surely he couldn't have run away again? With a growing feeling of dismay I realised that my little scheme could backfire devastatingly.

It wasn't until the tea had been made and poured

that I dared to raise the subject.

'How—' I asked diffidently. 'How is – er – Tiger?'

'Oh he's grand,' the little woman replied briskly. She glanced up at the clock on the mantelpiece. 'He should be back any time now, then you'll be able to see 'im.'

As she spoke, Sep raised a finger. 'Ah think ah can hear 'im now.'

He walked over and opened the door and our Oscar strode in with all his old grace and majesty. He took one look at Helen and leaped on to her lap. With a cry of delight she put down her cup and stroked the beautiful fur as the cat arched himself against her hand and the familiar purr echoed round the room.

'He knows me,' she murmured. 'He knows me.'

Sep nodded and smiled. 'He does that. You were good to 'im. He'll never forget ye, and we won't either, will we, mother?'

'No, we won't, Mrs Herriot,' his wife said as she applied butter to a slice of gingerbread. 'That was a kind thing ye did for us and I 'ope you'll come and see us all whenever you're near.'

'Well, thank you,' I said. 'We'd love to – we're often in Brawton.'

I went over and tickled Oscar's chin, then I turned again to Mrs Gibbons. 'By the way, it's after nine o'clock. Where has he been till now?'

She poised her butter knife and looked into space.

'Let's see, now,' she said. 'It's Thursday, isn't it? Ah yes, it's 'is night for the Yoga class.'

From *Vet in a Spin*

There are some people who simply cannot stand cats. They get into a sort of panic if a cat approaches them. They don't even have to *see* a cat, they can sense when there is one close to them, and they have to get out of the way. I know a lady who has this aversion to cats. One day she and her husband were dining in a restaurant. They were halfway through their meal when a cat walked through from the kitchens. It was the restaurant's Mouse Prevention Officer, but the lady and her husband had to leave. They couldn't wait to finish their meal, such was the lady's horror of cats. Some people say that cats are very well aware of people who dislike them and they will deliberately approach these people just for the satisfaction of putting them to flight.

On the other hand I can almost sense a house where there isn't a cat. A house without a cat seems to me to have something missing.

Of all the cats that have lived with me, three have been feral cats – that is to say, cats that have no home, no fixed address, who have lived wild, fending for themselves. Until they pluck up courage to walk into a house and ask to be taken in. Well, they hardly ask to be taken in, they simply say, 'This is not a bad place you've got here, don't happen to have a drop of milk, do you?' That usually settles it. After the first ceremonial saucer of milk they decide that this is the place for them.

The last feral cat that adopted me stayed until the day he died, and that was over eighteen years. Being a feral cat he was of course used to fending for himself, and most days he would bring a rabbit home. A small rabbit, it's true, but it made a substantial meal. Perhaps that is why he never bothered to hunt garden birds. It was a waste of time chasing a little bird – it wasn't even a bit of a snack. So he didn't mess about, he wanted a rabbit or nothing. He used to watch the birds at the bird-table and just blink his pale green eyes. He seemed to say 'Amusing and beautiful creatures, birds, but not for me, not for me.' To my knowledge he never caught a bird in his life but he kept the local rabbit population down most effectively.

In his spare time he appointed himself Mouse Prevention Officer to the house of his adoption and from time to time would make spot mouse checks. All cupboards had to be inspected, wardrobes looked under and all corners sniffed well out. You couldn't trust mice for a minute. The moment you turned your back they would be in. Only *he* knew when he was going to make a mouse check, only *he* knew when he was going to go out, to come in, to go to sleep, to sit on your lap. In fact he was a very cat-like cat. Like the Rum Tum Tugger.

The Rum Tum Tugger

T. S. Eliot

The Rum Tum Tugger is a Curious Cat:
If you offer him pheasant he would rather have grouse.
If you put him in a house he would much prefer a flat,
If you put him in a flat then he'd rather have a house.
If you set him on a mouse then he only wants a rat,
If you set him on a rat then he'd rather chase a mouse.
Yes the Rum Tum Tugger is a Curious Cat—
   And there isn't any call for me to shout it:
     For he will do
     As he do do
       And there's no doing anything about it!

The Rum Tum Tugger is a terrible bore:
When you let him in, then he wants to be out;
He's always on the wrong side of every door,
And as soon as he's at home, then he'd like to get about.
He likes to lie in the bureau drawer,
But he makes such a fuss if he can't get out.
Yes the Rum Tum Tugger is a Curious Cat—
   And it isn't any use for you to doubt it:
     For he will do
     As he do do
       And there's no doing anything about it!

The Rum Tum Tugger is a curious beast:
His disobliging ways are a matter of habit.
If you offer him fish then he always wants a feast;
When there isn't any fish then he won't eat rabbit.
If you offer him cream then he sniffs and sneers,
For he only likes what he finds for himself;
So you'll catch him in it right up to the ears,
If you put it away on the larder shelf.
The Rum Tum Tugger is artful and knowing,
The Rum Tum Tugger doesn't care for a cuddle;
But he'll leap on your lap in the middle of your sewing,
For there's nothing he enjoys like a horrible muddle.
Yes the Rum Tum Tugger is a Curious Cat—
    And there isn't any need for me to spout it:
      For he will do
      As he do do
        And there's no doing anything about it!

From *Old Possum's Book of Practical Cats*

It's very difficult once you have tamed a wild animal
to return it to the wild. Although it may still have its
strong natural instincts, it has been humanised and
trusts humans. This can cause difficulties. A friend of
mine, Norman Carr, lives in Africa. He reared two
male lion cubs. They grew to maturity and Norman
realised that he would have to return them to the wild
where they could fend for themselves. He went about
the rehabilitation carefully and methodically and the
two lions were gradually roaming further from home
and learning to hunt.

It was a very remote part of Africa. One day a motor
car came bumping along a track, making a horrible
noise. There was clearly something very wrong with
the engine. The driver stopped under a tree, got out
his tool-box and decided that he would repair the
engine there and then. He dragged his tool-box after
him as he crawled underneath his car. And there lying
on his back he set to work with screwdriver and
spanners.

Trying to repair a broken engine is most absorbing
work and the driver had been working away for about

twenty minutes, when he realised that he needed a larger spanner. He rolled on his side to get at his tool-box and there, lying beside him underneath the car, he saw an enormous lion just watching him working away. The man nearly died of fright.

Of course it was one of Norman Carr's tame lions who was very used to human beings. Seeing this human being lying down all on his own under a motor car, the lion thought that he would just keep him company. They were a couple of strange mechanics. And here are another strange couple, the Owl and the Pussy-cat.

The Owl and the Pussy-cat

Edward Lear

The Owl and the Pussy-cat went to sea
   In a beautiful pea-green boat,
They took some honey, and plenty of money,
   Wrapped up in a five-pound note.

The Owl looked up to the stars above,
   And sang to a small guitar,
'O lovely Pussy! O Pussy, my love,
   What a beautiful Pussy you are,
        You are,
        You are!
   What a beautiful Pussy you are!'

Pussy said to the Owl, 'You elegant fowl!
    How charmingly sweet you sing!
O let us be married! Too long we have tarried!
    But what shall we do for a ring?'
They sailed away, for a year and a day,
    To the land where the Bong-tree grows,
And there in a wood a Piggy-wig stood,
    With a ring at the end of his nose,
                His nose,
                His nose,
    With a ring at the end of his nose.

'Dear Pig, are you willing to sell for one shilling
    Your ring?' Said the Piggy, 'I will.'
So they took it away, and were married next day
    By the Turkey who lives on the hill.
They dined on mince, and slices of quince,
    Which they ate with a runcible spoon;
And hand in hand, on the edge of the sand,
    They danced by the light of the moon,
                The moon,
                The moon,
    They danced by the light of the moon.

From *The Complete Nonsense of Edward Lear*

People often write to me and say, 'Please, where can I get a grass snake?' or 'Please, where can I get a badger?' I have to say that I really don't know, and that in any case these creatures are much best left in the wild and not messed about and put in unnatural surroundings. Wild animals are for the wild. Stick to cats, dogs and the other animals that we have domesticated. Leave the wild ones alone, for tamed wild animals can often come to a very sticky end. And in many cases animals are taken from the wild just on a passing whim, and lead most unhappy lives as a result.

But in Phil Drabble's case it was much more than a whim – ever since he was a schoolboy he passionately wanted to own a badger. Oh yes, they can be tamed, and very amusing and lively animals they are, but you have got to know their characters, their habits, and the right way to look after them. Well, Phil Drabble reckoned that he could keep a badger and look after it properly, and so let's hear from him of how he found someone, a Mr Bert Gripton, who had a young badger and was prepared to let it go to a good home.

Bill Brock

Phil Drabble

I took it gently, almost reverently, from him and cupped it in my palms to hold it still whilst I examined it. I needn't have bothered. From above it looked a perfect miniature badger. Grey back and sides, and head with the characteristic black and white longitudinal stripes. He felt oddly smooth and warm. My first reaction was that he'd wet on my hands from fear but then I noticed that he was still blind. His two queer piggy little eyes had never seen the light of day. I turned him on his back to confirm what my sense of touch had already told me. Sure enough, 'he' was a little boar, but what did surprise me was that he was completely naked and bare underneath. What I had taken to be wetness was merely the warmth of his naked tummy.

That explained the almost tangible sense of doubt. Nobody in that room thought it possible to rear my cub. It was bad luck on that badger, of course, but at least it would put me in my place and show what I could do – if anything.

I accepted the unspoken challenge. I'd reared plenty of things before and I was determined to rear this one. More important than food was warmth. So when I got to the car I took the cub out of his bag of hay and stuffed him down my shirt against my warm tummy. He was just the size of a mole and, young as he was, his front feet were already powerful. I thought he was going to burrow through me before he got comfortable and many a time since I've wondered what the authorities would have thought if I'd had an accident going home and landed in hospital. It would almost have been worth it to watch the nurses' faces when they'd undone my shirt.

We got home safely though and my wife was as delighted as I. Only when we examined our new treasure by revealing electric light we found a long red scar where he had obviously only just escaped from the terriers with his life. It wasn't a very good start. I remembered the knowing looks at Gripton's and decided that the first thing to do was to christen him. No infant should be allowed to die unnamed. So he became Bloody Bill Brock.

Next we tried to feed him. It hadn't occurred to either of us that he would be so small, but now we saw the size of his diminutive mouth, a baby's teat was quite out of the question. How I wished for a cat with kittens which might have been persuaded to take on the dual role of giver of food and warmth.

We tried, singularly unsuccessfully, with a fountain-pen filler, but quickly gave up for the night. It is nearly always impossible to get young wild things to feed the first few hours they are in captivity. Provided they are reasonably strong, I never bother, but leave them to their sulks in the sure knowledge that hunger will bring them to their food within twenty-four hours.

What is essential, though, is warmth. At one time I

used to mess about filling hot-water bottles and re-placing them at regular intervals as they cooled off. I always found it quite hopeless. They were much too hot to start with and when they needed replenishing in the small hours I was usually too solidly asleep to do anything about it. And when I did eventually filter back into consciousness, my charge would be shivering and whimpering with cold.

By the time I acquired Bill Brock I had developed a much more efficient technique. I took the largest, flat-test cigarette tin I could find – I think it held 200 – and covered it with an ordinary sock. Inside the tin I put a 15-watt pigmy electric light bulb. The result was ideal. The bulb was just strong enough to produce a heat in the tin which was the perfect imitation of a mother's furry tummy. It had the incalculable advantage of being as warm in the morning as it was the night before. Placed in the bottom of a box it gives off the exact amount of heat which seems to be required by most young things, and I have used it for badgers and squirrels and rats and even a Siamese kitten.

In passing, I would mention that it once got me into severe hot water. I had been demonstrating on tele-vision how easy it is to rear chickens on my cigarette tin and pigmy bulb method. Knowing from bitter ex-perience how many people have nothing better to do than look in by the hour, for the express purpose of criticising what they see, I took normal evasive pre-cautions. I said that any children who thought of trying it should get their bulb and box fixed up by some knowledgeable grown-up. That, I thought, should put me in the clear. Not a bit of it. An irate electrician (probably a shop steward!) wrote to his local paper to say what a disgrace he thought it was that the BBC should employ amateur madmen to teach young innocents to electrocute themselves. And I spent the next few hours – which happened to be from about 10 p.m. till 2 in the morning – telling all the other newspapers what I'd really said.

Bill Brock, however, was not so critical. If he didn't like our baby food or our fountain-pen filler, at least he appreciated warmth and soft flannel. My wife had produced an old blanket with which we had completely lined a small packing-case. The cigarette tin with its little bulb was stuck under this blanket at one end of the box. Young Bill Brock, therefore, had blanket to lie on wherever he scrambled. So long as he stayed at one end on his tin, he had a warm blanket, as warm as if he was curled up with his litter-mates.

I think that first night was as restless for me as it was for him. Ever since I'd read those first natural history books at school my ambition had been to own a tame badger. Now I'd got him it seemed he was rather too young to do any good. If he died, I should have felt partly responsible for his being taken from his mother, for the receiver is deemed more guilty than the taker. I should also have felt extremely sheepish the next time I saw Bert Gripton who, I was certain, thought I wouldn't succeed.

Next morning it was cold and grey after a bitter night. But for once a warm bed didn't pull. I crept into the kitchen and slid a furtive hand quietly into the blanket in my packing-case. Joyously I discovered that the piggy little form on the tin was warm and wriggled and snuffled. So far, so good.

But he wouldn't take any baby food. We tried poking

a fountain-pen filler in his mouth but he only blew bubbles. We tried the baby's teat. As a last forlorn hope we dipped his nose in it. The only result was that we got him rather sticky and had to sponge him clean. Normally, I wouldn't have worried at all. So many wild things are wild and obstinate at first but act as though they have always been domesticated as soon as they feel the pangs of hunger. But my young Brock was different. The stakes were so much higher.

That night, when I got back from work, my wife was elated. She'd mixed some baby food at midday and he'd taken about a teaspoonful from the fountain-pen filler. I was all agog to try for myself. Taking the rug and badger, I settled down in an easy chair to fondle him until his milk food was warm. It was indeed a prophetic pose. For the next three or four weeks I was to spend at least two hours each day in this same chair whilst we really got to know each other. This first time, however, I wasn't very successful. Despite his hunger he hadn't taken to the flavour of his new food and his mother's breast must have been far more shapely and attractive than my glass tube. After about twenty minutes' struggle I succeeded in injecting a teaspoonful or so of nourishment into him and felt that he must have lost more strength in the struggle than he had gained in the meal. At night, things were but little better and we all went rather disheartened to bed.

When I got down next morning, he started to chatter and scream as soon as I touched him. He nuzzled my hand and was obviously nearly famished. The very smell of warm baby food sent him into such ecstasy that I was afraid he'd break the glass tube with sheer enthusiasm. His delight was short-lived. He sucked and spluttered his food down until he was partly filled and partly exhausted. Then his joy subsided into sleep, whilst I began my own breakfast with better appetite than I'd had since he came. My one worry was the danger of putting a rather frail glass tube into the mouth of such a tough young animal.

He was very difficult to start feeding from the bottle and it took a lot of experiment before he would accept a normal teat from a human baby's bottle. If the hole was too large, he would gulp the milk down so fast that he nearly choked and, if it was too small, he soon gave up trying.

One of the most critical things of all was the fact that it didn't take long for a teat to get shredded by such a vigorous youngster, but he would almost starve before he would accept a new teat with an unfamiliar smell. So I had to take great pains to try to get him using at least two teats, and I usually succeeded in 'breaking the next one in' by offering it to him first feed in the morning when his appetite was sharpest.

Even so, when he had taken the edge off his hunger, he would often stop feeding and sulk, so that I had to swap teats half-way through the feed and finish on one of his old favourites.

Each feed took about forty-five minutes so that we got to know each other pretty well before he was weaned, which undoubtedly helped to ensure that he stayed tame for the rest of his life. But forty-five minutes before work in the morning is a fair slice out of the day.

To badgers who have nothing else to do, I suppose, this wouldn't have mattered. I had to be shaved, breakfasted and nine miles away at work by nine in the morning, so that it affected me quite a lot. I fed him before breakfast, about six in the evening and just before I went to bed, and my wife fed him at midday. And, although we used to grumble, we were so elated by our success that our complaints were nothing but a matter of form.

Within four days, one piggy brown little eye opened, but not the other. He retained this evil-looking leering wink for the next couple of days and then suddenly he was transformed from fat immaturity into a perfect replica of the pictorial badger which ambles through the pages of books the world over.

Most young things grow very rapidly before they are weaned, and he was no exception. His belly became covered with black fur, he became clumsily playful as puppies do and his capacity for baby food increased even faster than his stature. As his mouth grew, it became possible to substitute the glass tube and doll's teat for a normal baby's bottle which was much easier to keep sterilised. But as he grew larger and needed more food at each meal, he seemed quite incapable of taking it faster, so that every meal still lasted about three-quarters of an hour. Despite this, he was most amusing to feed. If the hole was too large, so that the milk flowed freely, he choked and simply stopped feeding. If it was too small, he became simply furious and dived his head between his two front legs exactly as an adult badger does to dodge punishment. The result was dynamic. The teat stretched like a catapult, until the tortured rubber either pulled off the mouth of the bottle or slithered from the young animal's almost toothless jaws. In either case the result was the same. I got a lapful of sticky baby food.

From the very start, I used to let the dogs come whilst feeding was in progress so that they would get used to the sight and smell of badger in the house. My friends who came for an evening used to cock a knowing eyebrow when I slipped out of the room at about ten o'clock and returned laden with baby's bottle and towels and rug for protection. So many folk are so constipated with convention that they regard the idea of having a badger in the house as more than a little eccentric. They were patronising in their interest until, inevitably, they fell under the spell as soon as they really made Bill's acquaintance.

Then, quite suddenly, they would ask to be allowed first to stroke him, then to hold him and eventually to feed him. It would take some time for them to acquire the art of slipping his teat into a mouth rapidly disappearing between his forelegs. And each failure meant a spatter of gooey milk on waistcoats and dresses unsullied by anything less civilised than gin or sherry. I would snuggle back in my chair and watch with almost paternal pride, waiting for the cub to finish feeding and shuffle backwards a few steps. This was the signal that my guests were about to be sullied with something even more elemental than baby food, and I took a detached and objective interest in comparing their reactions. Most would giggle and dab self-consciously and return to their more conventional hobbies; occasionally, however, someone would become infected by my disease. Its symptoms are easily recognised. An interest in any wild thing is so absorbing that neither time, nor discomfort, nor convention matter by comparison.

This question of time is perhaps more important than any other single factor concerned with the taming and care of wild animals. A very great friend of mine, who is the best veterinary surgeon I know, once summed it up for me. 'The major requirement of a good vet,' he said, 'is to forget all about the clock.'

The critical time was over, but I have never found anything so difficult to wean as young Bill Brock. Normally, when most young animals I've been caring for obviously grow strong enough to fend for themselves, I give two bottle feeds a day and offer two more sloppy ones. Hunger is the finest sauce there is and, after the first day, there isn't usually much bother. I was so very proud of Bill, though, that I wouldn't take any chances. Besides, I knew that the longer he was bottle-fed the tamer he was likely to be. The result was that in May, when we wanted to go for a few days' holiday, he still wasn't properly weaned. All through March and April he'd spent over two hours a day on my lap or my wife's being fed from his bottle. It is true that by this time he was quicker drinking his food, but he was also more playful and agile. So what time we made up on the actual feed we lost again because we enjoyed playing as much as he did. He wrestled and bit exactly as a puppy does before he cuts his second teeth. Only he was rougher and 'harder mouthed' than any dog I've tried, except a Stafford Bull Terrier.

Our holiday was a mere week away, so something

had to be done. If we missed a feed and offered bread
and milk or bread and baby food, he squealed and
chattered with temper and stayed hungry. Then we discovered that half a round of bread all but floating in a
tin of warm milky food worked miracles. He smelt the
coveted liquid and nuzzled the spongy bread as if it
were the sow badger's belly and he was searching for a
teat. As he nuzzled he sucked, so that within a day or
so he was weaned and would feed perfectly satis-
factorily from a bowl. Now he no longer held any
terrors for the friend who had promised to care for
him while we were away. A week later, when we came
back, he seemed almost grown-up. He squealed and
chattered with delight to see me again, and I gave him
a bottle as a reunion feast.

Quite suddenly the problem arose of where to keep
him. I was very lucky because I lived in one of those
ugly red-brick box houses so beloved by the Vic-
torians. As a badge of their eminent respectability, they
had provided it with an excellent range of outbuildings,
including a stable. I'm never very fond of cold brick
floors to rear young animals, so I covered this stable
with a really thick layer of finely-chopped straw, and I
kept the same packing-case sleeping-box, with its false
bottom to accommodate the little bulb for heating it.
In order that he could gradually be weaned of artificial
heat as well as his bottle, I supplied a spare sleeping-
box with more straw and comfort, switching off the
current in his old one during the daytime. Only as the
weather warmed and he took to the more softly padded
(if cooler) box, did I cease heating the original one.

The hard work was over now and the fun began.

Our young badger had spent so much time with us that he was completely unafraid. He came out in the garden after tea and gambolled round, either with us or with the dogs. When he got excited, he chattered and squealed and his long coat stood on end like a golliwog so that, quite suddenly, he looked twice the size and very formidable.

But he wasn't a very good gardener. While he was the size of a small cat it hadn't been so bad, but by the end of June he was bigger than Muffit, my hunt terrier, and literally ploughed through the flower borders, leaving them with a morning-after-the-tornado look. I couldn't see that there was much more left to spoil, and 'Anyway,' I told my wife, 'everyone down the road had got a barrow-load of flowers in the garden but we're the only ones with a badger.' It didn't work. Bill and I were asked to go and play in someone else's yard.

Across the road was a field belonging to my father, so we went there. On the way we were constantly stopped. I was generally regarded as slightly 'odd' by the neighbours, so they had no qualms about accosting me to see 'what I'd got this time'. They mostly thought Bill was 'pretty' or 'quaint' and made the same sort of clucking remarks about him that they would have made about the latest baby in the road or, at any rate, about anything as unusual as twins. And one good lady was quite certain he was dangerous and wondered if her children were safe.

Once the field gate was shut behind us, all was quiet and peaceful. I discovered that, wherever I walked, Bill Brock followed as close to my heels as a trained spaniel, for the very simple reason that he was simply terrified of being lost. He was so short-sighted that he couldn't see me five yards away unless I moved. Often, when the dogs were playing with him, they'd all run 50 or 100 yards across the field, and then the dogs would put on a sprint and leave him standing. His look of horror was eloquent.

With his legs four-square and rigid he'd stand stock-still and petrified, straining every muscle to catch the faintest sound to indicate which way to run to me for protection. Sometimes I'd tease him and freeze as still and silent as he was. Seconds would grow into minutes and neither of us would give way. Then he'd begin to move. It was a most unexpected gait and almost impossible to detect the precise instant when he slid from his statuesque immobility. A few minutes before, when he'd been playing with the dogs, there had been a puffing and pounding of feet enough to sound like a herd of cattle stampeding. His instinctive caution had been conquered by his tameness.

The moment he was lost, he reverted to a wild animal which could steal over the ground as smoothly and as silently as a shadow.

From *A Weasel in my Meatsafe*

I am always amazed by the loyalty and obedience a guide dog has for its master. This next story really impresses me, as it shows the astonishing intelligence of a guide dog, even to the point of *disobeying* her owner's command. It is written by a blind girl who has just met Emma, her guide dog. She is staying at the special centre where Brian is training dog and owner to work together.

Emma

Sheila Hocken

My first walk with Emma came that afternoon, and it was immediately evident why we had to have a month's training with the dogs. Although Emma took to me, and we got on well together, she would not do a thing I told her. She would obey no one but Brian. Attachment and obedience to me would clearly come only with training.

I put Emma's harness on, and we started off down a quiet road near the centre. Brian was standing next to us. He gave the command to go forward, but before he even got the '—ward' bit out we were off, several miles down the road it seemed, and I was galloping along, hanging on grimly to the harness.

'I'll never keep this up,' I managed to gasp.

'Oh, you'll soon get used to it,' said Brian. 'You'll get fitter as you go along. The trouble is you've been accustomed to walking so slowly.'

A guide-dog's pace apparently averages about four miles an hour. This compares with an ordinary sighted person's two to three miles an hour. So what kind of speed I used to achieve before, I have no idea, but it was obviously not competitive even with that of the snail population. At last I began to settle down to the fast rhythm, and was just beginning to think I might

enjoy it after all, when, without any warning whatsoever, Emma stopped. I was off the pavement before I
could pull up. Emma had sat down on the kerb, and
I heard Brian laughing.

'Don't go without your dog, that's Lesson Number
One,' Brian said. 'If you go sailing on when she stops
at the kerb, you'll get run over. She stops, you stop.'

'Well, I didn't know she was going to stop, did I?
And you didn't tell me.'

'No, you're right. But you've got to learn to follow
your dog.'

Brian was about twenty-eight at the time, very pleasant and with a great sense of humour. I imagined him
good-looking with fair hair and glasses. I liked him
especially because he refused to make concessions to
our blindness. He expected us to be independent.
Rather than mop us up, and say, 'There, there,' when
we fell off the kerb, he would turn it into a joke, which
was the best medicine. At least it was for me. It certainly made me get up and think, 'Right. I'll show you
who can be a good guide-dog owner.'

So on this occasion I got back behind Emma, took
up the harness again, and said, 'What next?'

'You've got to cross this road. First you listen for
any traffic. If it's quiet, you give Emma the command
to go forward.'

When I could hear no traffic, this is what I did. But
nothing happened.

Brian said, 'She knows that you're behind her and
not me. You've got to encourage her, to make her want
to take you over the road.'

'Good girl, Emma,' I said, 'there's a clever dog.' And

after a little more of this persuasion, and the word 'Forward', thrown in from time to time, she finally took me across the road.

Crossing the road with a guide-dog is a matter of teamwork: whatever you do, you do it together. I have met sighted people with such weird ideas about this. Either they think the dogs are not very clever, but just wear the harness to show their owner is blind – a sort of plea for help – or they think the dogs are superhuman, and the blind people idiots who are being taken round for a walk rather as other people take their dogs. The importance of partnership, or even its existence, never seems to occur to most people. My job when crossing a road was to listen and Emma's was to look. Only when I could hear nothing should I give her the command to cross. But if I was wrong in my assessment of the traffic, and she could see something coming, she would wait until it was clear.

Guide-dogs are taught to stop and sit down at every kerb and wait for the next command. The four basic commands are, 'Right', 'Left', 'Back', and 'Forward'. And you have to position yourself with your dog so that you give her every opportunity to obey the right command. For instance, when the command to go forward is given, it is accompanied by an indication in that direction with the arm. It is also important to keep talking to the dog, and Brian reminded me of this on our first walk, just after we had crossed the road.

'Don't stop talking, or Emma'll think you've fallen asleep.'

'What do I say?' I asked rather stupidly.

'It doesn't matter, as long as you make it interesting.

'Tell her what you had for breakfast if you like.'

So there I was, galloping along a street in Leamington discussing bacon and eggs with a chocolate-coloured Labrador. Brian went on, 'You're working together, and if you stop talking, she'll stop working. You've got to keep her interest. She's a dog, and there are lots of nice, interesting smells all round, and things passing that you can't see. So unless you talk to her, she'll get distracted, and stop to sniff a lamp post.' I was quite hoarse by the time we had finished our first walk together.

I owe a great deal to Brian, not only for his training, but also for matching Emma and me together. His assessment of all he knew about us resulted in an inspired pairing, as time was to prove.

One day I remember asking him where Emma came from. What I really meant was, how did the centres come by the guide-dogs? Brian explained that they came to Leamington, or one of the other centres, after being puppy-walked. The Guide-Dog Association has a big breeding and puppy-walking centre at Tollgate House, near Warwick. They own a number of brood bitches and stud dogs that are let out to people as pets, because, naturally, a permanent kennel life is not desirable, and living with a family is a much happier arrangement. At the same time the Association controls which dog should mate with which. When the litters come along, it picks the dogs or bitches required for training. At about eight weeks old, a puppy undergoes various tests to see if it is basically bold and friendly, and capable of being trained as a guide-dog. Dogs bred in this way form about sixty per cent of the total, and there are now about two thousand guide-dog owners in the country. The remaining forty per cent come to the Association either by purchase or donation from breeders or private individuals. But the rejection rate is high. Dogs are kept on approval for about three weeks to see if they are suitable. If they're not, they're returned to their owners. The dogs chosen are usually female, because the male dog has a rather different outlook and nature, including a territorial instinct, and is not as tractable as the female, who in any case is spayed for the purposes of being a guide-dog. About seventy per cent of the dogs used are Labradors, like Emma – though I prefer to think she is unique, even among Labradors – and the remainder Alsatians, Collies, Golden Retrievers, and crosses from all of these.

Once the selection is made, the puppies go to people called puppy-walkers, who live around the training centres, and give homes to potential guide-dogs for about a year. In this time they have to teach the dog the basics. The dogs learn how to be well-mannered and clean in the house, to keep off furniture, not to beg for food, and to obey commands such as 'Sit', 'Stay', 'Down', 'Come', and so on. They are taught to walk on a lead, but not at heel, because of course they will eventually be required to walk in front of a blind man or woman. In general, the puppy-walkers are expected to take the dog everywhere with them, so that the dog is not shy of traffic, buses or trains, or the sort of sudden noises that sometimes occur in the street, such as pneumatic drills. They are also specifically instructed to take the dogs shopping. During this phase the puppy grows up and becomes used to urban life, and at the same time should remain bold and friendly.

At this point, Brian told me, they come to the centres for guiding training, which lasts about five months. The puppy-walkers do a wonderful job. I couldn't do it myself: have a dog for a year, then part with it; then have another, and see it go, and so on, and I really admire those who do so much to forge the first essential link between dog and blind person.

Naturally, when Brian told me all this, I wanted to know who had puppy-walked Emma, and he said, 'Someone called Paddy Wansborough. She's a marvellous woman. She's given nine or ten dogs to the Association after puppy-walking them. In fact, Emma wasn't bred by the Association. She was given to Paddy as a puppy, given her basic year, and then donated to the Association.'

I determined that one of the first things I would do when I got home would be to contact Paddy Wansborough.

Next day, I was out with Emma again. As the training progressed I gradually got more used to her. We used a mini-bus to get us about Leamington, and this played a big part in the training, because it taught us how to use public transport. When we were on the bus and the dogs under the seats, I heard a great bellow from Brian, 'I can see two brown paws sticking out.' Brown paws, I thought, that must be Emma.

He went on, 'Do you want somebody to stand on her?'

'No, of course I don't.'

'Well, do something about it.'

I began to wonder if my first impressions of Brian

had been wrong. But though he was shouting at me a lot, he must have guessed what I was thinking.

'No one else is going to tell you these things, Sheila. If you don't learn here, Emma'll be the one that suffers, not you.'

My trust in Emma grew daily, but I really knew she had transferred her affections from Brian to me on about the tenth day of my stay at the centre. Up to then, she had always slept until morning in her dog-bed on the other side of the room. But on this particular evening, she refused to go to her bed. Instead, she curled up on the floor as near to my pillow as she could get. I felt then that we had made it. We were a team, each needing the other's company. I woke the following morning with an odd sensation. It felt as if there were a steamroller on my chest. Emma was sitting on top of me, pushing with her nose, telling me, I have no doubt at all, that it was time for us both to get up. She was full of life and exuberance, and could not wait to start the day. When I did get up, I could hear her shake herself in anticipation, and stand wagging her tail near the door.

One of the centre's ingenious ways of familiarising us with the day's programme was by using tactile maps. Pavements, buildings, and so on were raised on a wooden map of Leamington, so we could feel our way over the routes beforehand, right down to the zebra crossings and the bus stops. Emma would find these things for me, but I had to be in the right road, and the map helped enormously to make sure we did not miss our way. Our walks became more and more compli-cated, and Brian would try to find places where there were road works, to ensure we had mastered the business of getting round them, as well as other obstacles. Bus trips and shopping expeditions were also in the curriculum, and I really enjoyed shopping with Emma. She would not only find the shop, but also take me up to the counter. I began to forget I was blind. No one fussed round me any longer. They were all too interested in Emma.

But things did not always go smoothly. I was not keen on the obstacle course we had to practise. Emma always reacted very quickly, and usually I was not fast enough to follow. She would see the obstacle, assess it, and take a snap decision which way to go. Before I knew what was happening she would have changed course to one side or the other, and I would be left in a trail of harness and confusion. Brian always seemed to be on hand when I made mistakes, even if I thought he was following some other student. I would suddenly hear a great shout: 'When your dog jumps, you jump.'

It was easier said than done. On occasions like this, Emma would lose confidence and sit down immediately. It was almost as if she were saying, 'It's no good me doing my bit, if all you can do is to trail behind and finish up in a heap.' Literally the only way I could get her back to work again was to apologise and promise to do better next time.

It was while we were doing the obstacle course that I learned one of Emma's aversions. It came to our turn and we were going through the obstacles fairly well. All at once Emma shot off like a rocket, and I felt myself being taken at right angles up a steep grass bank. As we went, I heard Brian hysterical with laughter.

When we finally came to a stop, I said rather breathlessly, 'What was all that about? Whatever did she do that for?'

'Oh, it's Napoleon.'

'Napoleon? What do you mean, Napoleon?' I thought Brian had suddenly gone out of his mind.

'You know,' he said, 'the cat. Napoleon, the cat.'

'Oh,' I said. But I still did not know why Emma had shot up the bank.

Brian, still laughing, explained that Emma could not stand cats. She knew better than to chase them, but if she saw one, she would take off in the opposite direction – the opposite direction in this case having been the steep grassy bank. Still, Brian did congratulate me on my alacrity and speed in following, and promised to keep us in mind if there was ever a guide-dog expedition to Everest. At the same time, I thought that the only way to cure Emma of her dislike of cats would be to get one, and I put that on my list of resolutions for when I got home.

That evening as we were sitting in the lounge, Brian came in and we laughed again about Emma and the cat. Then I asked him something that fascinated me more and more the longer the course went on. How did they train the dogs to accomplish the amazing things they did for us? I knew a little about dog training from the experience I had had with them, but I could not fathom some of the dogs' abilities. After all, it is a fairly simple matter to train a dog to sit at a kerb every time but how do you train them to disobey you? I asked Brian, 'For instance, I told Emma to go forward yesterday, when I hadn't heard a car coming, and she wouldn't go because she'd seen one. How on earth do you train them to do that?'

Brian replied, 'Once you've got a dog basically trained, and you're waiting to cross the road, you see a car coming and tell the dog to go forward. The dog, naturally, obeys immediately, but you don't move, and the car – other trainers drive them for these exercises – hoots, and makes a lot of noise, and the dog comes back on the pavement; by repetition of this sort of thing the dog is conditioned to associate the moving vehicle with danger, and therefore, despite all instinct to obey, refuses to move even when the command is given. Of course, only fairly intelligent dogs will respond like this, and that's why we have to be very stringent with our tests of character and aptitude to begin with.'

'What about obstacles?' I asked.

Brian explained that the principle behind teaching dogs not to walk their owners into obstacles was to get the dog to associate an obstacle with displeasure – to use a mild word – and also distress. A start is made with something simple such as a post. The dog walks the trainer into the post, is immediately stopped, the post is banged to draw attention to it, and the right way, allowing room, is shown. The next time a forceful 'NO' is shouted when the post is collided with, and the right way is shown again. So by repetition the dog eventually gets the message, and at the same time, the range of obstacles is extended to include the most frequent pavement obstacles of all, people.

It sounded simple in a way, but I knew a lot of hard work and talented training went into all this. The trainers, Brian told me, worked with a blindfold on when they considered the dogs had reached a certain standard of proficiency. They did this for about a fortnight to create real working conditions for the dogs, and give them confidence through working with someone they knew.

It was interesting to hear Brian explain it all, and particularly, in the light of what followed in the last stage of the course, the disobedience part. We were nearing the end of our month at Leamington, and went out once more in the mini-bus. Emma's paws, by now, were always well tucked away. Brian told us we were going to the railway station as a final test.

I have always loathed railway stations because of the noise, the hundred and one different obstacles, and the general sense of bustle which, if you are blind, is scaring. I got to dislike them so much I would never go into one still less travel by train, even if there were a sighted person to take me. But Brian was adamant. 'Well, you know, you've got to get used to it. You might want to go by rail one day, or meet somebody off a train, and you've got Emma to guide you now. She knows her way around. There's nothing to it.'

I was not convinced. We got to the station, and I put Emma's harness on. Brian said, 'Right. I'll just go and park. You go in; Emma knows the way. I'll be with you in a minute or two.'

Emma took me through the doors, down a couple of flights of steps, in and out between people on the platform and sat down. I had no idea where I was. I just stood and waited for Brian. He was there within a couple of minutes. 'Right,' he said, 'Emma's sitting bang on the edge of the platform. There's about a six-foot drop in front of you to the railway line. Now tell her to go forward.'

I was petrified, and could feel my spine tingle. 'You must be joking,' I said.

'No, go on. Tell her to go forward.'

I stood there, not knowing what to do. This really was a terrible test. Dare I do it? I was so scared, I felt sick. In that moment I really did not want a guide-dog. Everything I had heard about them, all the training we had done, all I felt about Emma flashed through my mind, and it meant nothing. I just wanted, there and then, to lay the harness handle on Emma's back, and leave, get out, escape, anything. But in a sort of hoarse whisper, I heard myself saying, 'Forward.'

Immediately, up she got, and almost in the same motion pushed herself in front of my legs. Then she started pushing me back, right away from the edge of the platform.

I have never felt so ashamed in all my life. I felt about an inch tall. How could I possibly have been so doubting, so unworthy of Emma? I was utterly humiliated. Brian said, 'There you are. I told you Emma would look after you, whatever you do. Whatever you tell her to do, if there's any danger in front of you, she'll push you away.'

So that was it. We had made it. The sense of freedom was incredible. I got over my awful feelings of shame, because I sensed that Emma understood and forgave. That afternoon I walked with her down the Parade in Leamington, the busy main road, crowded with shoppers. I walked with a great big smile on my face, weaving in and out of all those people, and feeling: I don't care if you can *see* I'm blind. I can see too: I've got Emma, and she's all I need.

All too soon the day came when we were to go home, Emma and I. It was, oddly enough, very sad. It happened to be raining – pouring down – and the weather matched my mood. Even though I could not see the rain, I felt very grey and depressed. I hated the idea of having to leave the centre and all the friends I had made. Even more, I really did not want to go home, although I now had Emma, and kept trying to convince myself that things back in Nottingham were *bound* to be different. I was afraid that somehow I might be enveloped in the old ways again, despite Emma. I had not yet grasped to what an enormous extent she was about to change my life. I still had to learn to put my confidence in her.

Heavy with misgivings, I left Leamington with Emma on her harness beside me. The two of us arrived in Nottingham, were met and taken home. Once home, I let Emma off the lead and took off her harness: she went wild. Everyone was immediately taken with her. She bounded all over the place, through every room, round and round; I could hear her tearing about, sending rugs flying, stopping to sniff each chair and table leg. The air swished to the wagging of her tail, and resounded with her snortings and sniffings. This, she obviously realised, was where she was going to live. It was such a different Emma from the sober responsible animal on the harness, and for the first time I appreciated that there were two distinct sides to her character: one when she was working, and in charge of me, and the other when she was off the harness, totally joyous, full of fun and energy, and as far from any sense of responsibility as a clown. My misgivings began to evaporate.

Emma and I started to go to work together as soon as we were settled again. At that time I lived in Carlton, on one side of Nottingham, and I worked right over the other side, the Bulwell side of the city. I had to catch two buses with a walk across the Market Square in the middle of Nottingham in between. The terminus for the first bus was at the bottom of our road, so that part was easy. Emma trotted down the road with her tail in the air – I could feel it brushing my hand as we went along – and, at the same time, I began to learn how sensitive it was possible to be, via the harness, to what she was doing. Through it I could tell whether her ears were up or down, whether she was turning her head left or right, and all sorts of little movements.

We found the stop, and from that moment Emma loved going on buses. It was not just the bus itself, however. One important factor was the admiration she received that morning, and every time we got on a bus henceforth: 'Oh, what a lovely dog. Oh, what a beautiful colour.' And so on. I could sense Emma basking in the glory. She had picked the second seat on the right for me. For some reason, this was the place she always chose on this particular bus. I sat down, and Emma went under the seat. Strangely, this was the only bus on which she had such a preference: it always had to be the same one. After we had been going to

J.M.A.S.B—5

work together for about three weeks, we were nearing the bus one morning when I began to pick up the sound of a great commotion going on inside it. As we came alongside I could hear a woman's muffled shout: 'You'll have to get up you know. You can't sit there, I tell you it's Emma's seat. Come on – they'll be here in a minute.'

On other buses, Emma simply went for any empty seat, preferably – in the winter at least – one near the heaters. But since we normally travelled in the rush-hour the buses, apart from our first one, were very often full, so she had to use a different technique. She would drag me along the aisle, nosing everyone else out of the way if there were standing passengers, decide on where she wanted us to sit, then stare at whoever was sitting there until they gave way. To be fair, they normally gave the seat up very quickly, and before the bus was in an uproar. This, of course, appealed to the exhibitionist in Emma. When she was sure she had got her audience, she would turn to me, lay her head across my knee, looking, I imagined, specially devoted and possibly a little pathetic. By this time the entire bus was hers.

But to get back to that first morning. When I walked into the office there was a reception committee waiting. While everyone said 'Hello' to me, they were clearly more interested in seeing what Emma was like. Emma once again responded with great delight, and when I had taken her harness off, took it round, her tail wagging, to show everyone in turn.

So she was a hit straight away, and when the others had gone she inspected her basket, played for a while with a rubber toy I had brought with me to occupy her, then settled down. The telephone had already started going, and soon it was like old times – with the tremendous difference of that reassuring sleeping form under my desk. The morning went on, and in a lull, thinking what a good quiet dog Emma was being, I put my hand down to pat her head. But, where her head should have been, there was nothing. I felt round in a wider circle. Emma had disappeared! I immediately got up and went to feel if my office door was open; sure enough, it was. I called her. No response. All sorts of anxieties began to crowd in on me. Had she got out? What if she had gone into the street? What if she were lost ... what ... then I heard the sound of paws coming down the corridor. Thank goodness. In came Emma. 'Emma,' I said, 'where *have* you been?' Her reply was to push something into my lap. I did not want to believe my fingers. It was a purse. I was horrified. 'Emma! Where did you get that from?' Her reply this time was to do her tattoo bit, bouncing up and down on her forelegs, and swishing me furiously with her tail. The message was clear: 'How about that for brilliance! I've brought you somebody's purse.' Fleetingly, the thought of a four-legged Artful Dodger came to mind. I took the purse from her, and hoped that someone would come and claim it, and accept my excuses.

The owner concerned eventually found out what had happened, and came to claim the purse. But no one would believe that I had not taught Emma to perform the trick, which did nothing to ease my mind about the prospect of the afternoon, or indeed of continuing to work for Industrial Pumps. It was a relief to take Emma out of the office for a run in the local park. This was something I had decided I must do every day. Since she worked hard it was only fair that she should have a free run whenever possible.

I sat myself on a bench with my sandwiches, let her off the lead, and she went charging across the grass. I soon heard barking in the distance, and recognised Emma. But every so often she would come back to me, touch my hands with her nose, and then scamper off again. It was something that she never failed to do whenever we went to the park from then on. She was reassuring me: 'I'm here, and I haven't forgotten you.'

That afternoon I sat down at the switchboard, and, in between calls, waited uneasily for the sound of Emma bringing me another gift. But she settled down and slept, and after that did not bring any more presents – at least, not in the office. Perhaps it was her way of making a mark, and returning her welcome. Whatever it was, I was pleased it was over.

The first week went by very happily. Travelling to and from work, in fact, became easier every day. I did not have to give Emma all the lefts and rights in the Square because she soon began to take me straight to the right road and across to the forty-three bus stop. I started to appreciate, and this was something that established itself firmly as time went on, that Emma had only to take any route once and she knew it. I had no sooner discovered this than I found there was a drawback in having such an intelligent dog.

About the middle of the second week we set off for work as usual. I merely said to Emma that we were going to work, and, by now, knew she could do this without any corrections or promptings. We got our first bus, and reached the Market Square. Everything was fine. But when we got to the first road to cross in the Square, Emma sat down instead of going forward. I listened for traffic, and when I thought it was clear, told her to go forward. But she would not move. She simply continued to sit. I could not understand what was going on. I thought that perhaps I had misjudged the traffic, so when it was quiet I told her again. Still she would not go forward. Instead, she got up and turned right, and started taking me along the pavement. 'Emma,' I said, rather desperately, as I was being dragged along, 'where are you taking me? Where's the bus stop? Come on. Bus stop . . .' But no, she would not listen, or if she did listen she certainly did not take any notice. We went on, across a road, made a sharp left turn, and crossed another road. Then she sat down again. I had no idea where we were. I had completely lost my sense of direction, and was utterly confused about the pattern I had to keep in my mind in order to reach the bus stop; this was the equivalent of the checks that sighted people, probably uncon- sciously, make when they are getting from A to B: right at St Mary's Church, past W. H. Smith's, left at the Royal Oak, and so on.

I was not only disappointed in Emma, but slightly upset and annoyed with her as well. 'Emma,' I said crossly, 'we shall be late for work.' How do you tell the boss that it was the dog who made you late? Thinking back, it must have looked a rather comic scene to any- one passing by. 'Excuse me,' I said as the next footsteps approached, 'can you tell me how to get to the forty-three bus stop, please?' There was a silence for a second or two, during which time I thought: they don't know, we really are lost. Then a man's voice, obviously puzzled, said, 'Forty-three bus stop? You're *at* the forty-three bus stop. Your dog's at the foot of the post.' I was relieved, astonished, and utterly baffled. We got on the bus when it came along, and I put the incident out of my mind. Until the following morning.

This time Emma went left instead of right, crossed another road, turned right, crossed a further road, walked along and sat down. We were at the forty-three bus stop again. I was unnerved, but by now getting used to the feeling. At work, I asked Carol, a friend who I knew came to the office via the Market Square, if there were any roadworks on the route I had originally mapped out. She said no, and no new building either, or any kind of obstruction.

I was totally at a loss. I thought and thought, and then the only possible explanation came to me: Emma, having learnt a route, became bored with having to follow it every day. So she invented variations. From then on she found a series of routes round the Market Square quite independently of any guidance from me, and chose one of them every day. I soon became resigned to this and got up ten minutes earlier just to allow for Emma's possibly making a mistake. But, of course, she never did.

From *Emma and I*

Mice

Rose Fyleman

I think mice
Are rather nice.

   Their tails are long,
   Their faces small,
   They haven't any
   Chins at all.
   Their ears are pink,
   Their teeth are white,
   They run about
   The house at night.
   They nibble things
   They shouldn't touch
   And no one seems
   To like them much.

But I think mice
Are nice.

In the introduction to this book we talked about
'Horse Sense' and I said that Horse Sense could mean
that if you've done a certain thing once then it will be
reasonably safe to do it again. On the other hand if
you do a certain thing and you get hurt or frightened
doing it, you will think twice before you do that thing
again. I remember we once had some police horses in
the *Animal Magic* studio to demonstrate how they
could remain calm and collected even when we fired
off revolvers, started smoke bombs and blew trumpets
in their ears. They could put up with that all right, but
what the police officers had to do first of all was to
prove to them that the surface of the studio floor was
not dangerous.

Television studio floors have to be absolutely flat
and very shiny so that the cameras can move about
smoothly. The horses were suspicious of such a surface, never having met one like it before. You could
tell by the look in their eyes and the way they rattled
the bits in their mouths. But the officers spoke softly

and coaxed them and they walked around the studio very carefully. And having done that once and found everything was all right they performed with every confidence.

Horses are most sensitive creatures and very often a horse that has been badly treated when young will turn into a 'brute'. I have a friend who specialises in dealing with problem horses and he has to find out, if he can, just what has gone wrong with the horse. It may had have a bad time when being broken in; it may have been in the charge of a rough and clumsy stable lad; it may have been bullied into doing things that it hated doing. It takes a lot of patience and time to pacify a horse and gain its confidence. A horse that has no confidence in its handler is a most difficult horse.

But horses, like human beings, vary a great deal in character. In the story *My Friend Flicka* the yearling Flicka doesn't have a very good start in life. She lives on a ranch in America where all the young horses roam free until they are caught and broken in. Rob Mc-Laughlin, who owns the ranch, lets his son Ken choose his own yearling horse. Ken chooses Flicka, although his father thinks she is too wild to be tamed. She has already been caught and managed to escape. But Ken won't listen to his father's objections: he wants Flicka. Here we join Ken, his father, his brother Howard and the ranch hands Tim and Ross as they try to catch the yearlings, including Flicka. But Flicka is determined not to be caught a second time.

Flicka

Mary O'Hara

When Ken opened his eyes next morning and looked out he saw that the house was wrapped in fog. There had been no rain at all since the day a week ago when the wind had torn the 'sprinkling system' to pieces and blown all the tattered clouds away. That was the day he had found Flicka. And it had been terribly hot since then. They had hardly been able to stand the sun out on the terrace. They had gone swimming in the pool every day. On the hills, the grass was turning to soft tan.

Now there were clouds and they had closed down. After a severe hot spell there often came a heavy fog, or hail, or even snow.

Standing at the window, Ken could hardly see the pines on the Hill opposite. He wondered if his father would go after the yearlings in such a fog as this – they wouldn't be able to see them; but at breakfast McLaughlin said there would be no change of plan. It was just a big cloud that had settled down over the ranch – it would lift and fall – perhaps up on Saddle Back it would be clear.

They mounted and rode out.

The fog lay in the folds of the hills. Here and there a bare summit was in sunshine, then a little farther on came a smother of cottony white that soaked the four riders to the skin and hung rows of moonstones on the whiskers of the horses

It was hard to keep track of each other. Suddenly Ken was lost – the others had vanished. He reined in Shorty and sat listening. The clouds and mist rolled around him. He felt as if he were alone in the world.

A bluebird, colour of the deep blue wild delphinium that dots the plains, became interested in him, and perched on a bush nearby; and as he started Shorty forward again, the bluebird followed along, hopping from bush to bush.

The boy rode slowly, not knowing in which direction to go. Then, hearing shouts, he touched heels to Shorty and cantered, and suddenly came out of the fog and saw his father and Tim and Ross.

'There they are!' said McLaughlin, pointing down over the curve of the hill. They rode forward and Ken could see the yearlings standing bunched at the bottom, looking up, wondering who was coming. Then a huge coil of fog swirled over them and they were lost to sight again.

McLaughlin told them to circle around, spread out fanwise on the far side of the colts, and then gently bear down on them so they would start towards the ranch. If the colts once got running in this fog, he said, there'd be no chance of catching them.

The plan worked well; the yearlings were not so frisky as usual, and allowed themselves to be driven in the right direction. It was only when they were on the County Road, and near the gate where Howard was watching, that Ken, whose eyes had been scanning the bunch, as they appeared and disappeared in the fog, realised that Flicka was missing.

McLaughlin noticed it at the same moment, and as Ken rode towards his father, McLaughlin turned to him and said, 'She's not in the bunch.'

They sat in silence a few moments while McLaughlin planned the next step. The yearlings, dispirited by the fog, nibbled languidly at the grass by the roadside. McLaughlin looked at the Saddle Back and Ken looked too, the passionate desire in his heart reaching out to pierce the fog and the hillside and see where Flicka had hidden herself away. Had she been with the bunch when they first were found? Had she stolen away through the fog? Or hadn't she been there in the be-ginning? Had she run away from the ranch entirely, after her bad experience a week ago? Or – and this thought made his heart drop sickeningly – had she per-haps died of the hurts she had received when she broke out of the corral; was she lying stark and riddled with ants and crawling things on the breast of one of those hills?

McLaughlin looked grim. 'Lone wolf – like her mother,' he said. 'Never with the gang. I might have known it.'

Ken remembered what the Colonel had said about the Lone Wolf type – it wasn't good to be that way.

'Well, we'll drive the yearlings back up,' said Rob finally. 'No chance of finding her alone. If they happen to pass anywhere near her she's likely to join them.'

They drove the yearlings back. Once over the first hill, the colts got running and soon were out of sight. The fog closed down again so that Ken pulled up, unable to see where he was going, unable to see his father, or Ross or Tim.

He sat listening, astonished that the sound of their hoofs had been wiped out so completely. Again he seemed alone in the world.

The fog lifted in front of him and showed him that he stood at the brink of a sharp drop, almost a precipice, though not very deep. It led down into a semicircular pocket on the hillside which was fed by a spring; there was a clump of young cottonwoods, and a great bank of clover dotted with small yellow blossoms.

In the midst of the clover stood Flicka, quietly feasting. She had seen him before he saw her and was watching him, her head up, clover sticking out of both sides of her mouth, her jaws going busily.

At sight of her, Ken was incapable of either thought or action.

Suddenly from behind him in the fog, he heard his father's low voice, 'Don't move—'

'How'd she get in there?' said Tim.

'She scrambled down this bank. And she could scramble up again, if we weren't here. I think we've got her,' said McLaughlin.

'Other side of that pocket the ground drops twenty feet sheer,' said Tim. 'She can't go down there.'

Flicka had stopped chewing. There were still stalks of clover sticking out between her jaws, but her head was up and her ears pricked, listening, and there was a tautness and tension in her whole body.

Ken found himself trembling too.

'How're you going to catch her, Dad?' he asked in a low voice.

'I kin snag her from here,' said Ross, and in the same breath McLaughlin answered, 'Ross can rope her. Might as well rope her here as in the corral. We'll spread out in a semi-circle above this bank. She can't get up past us, and she can't get down.'

They took their positions and Ross lifted his rope off the horn of his saddle.

Ahead of them, far down below the pocket, the yearlings were running. A whinny or two drifted up, and the sound of their hoofs, muffled by the fog.

Flicka heard them too. Suddenly she was aware of danger. She leaped out of the clover to the edge of the precipice which fell away down the mountainside towards where the yearlings were running. But it was too steep and too high. She came straight up on her hind legs with a neigh of terror, and whirled back towards the bank down which she had slid to reach the pocket. But on the crest of it, looming uncannily in the fog, were four black figures – she screamed, and ran around the base of the bank.

Ken heard Ross's rope sing. It snaked out just as Flicka dived into the bank of clover. Stumbling she went down and for a moment was lost to view.

'Goldarn—' said Ross, hauling in his rope, while Flicka floundered up and again circled her small prison, hurling herself at every point, only to realise that there was no way out.

She stood over the precipice, poised in despair and frantic longing. There drifted up the sound of the colts running below. Flicka trembled and strained over the brink – a perfect target for Ross, and he whirled his lariat again. It made a vicious whine.

Ken longed for the filly to escape the noose – yet he

longed for her capture. Flicka reared up, her delicate forefeet beat the air, then she leaped out; and Ross's rope fell short again as McLaughlin said, 'I expected that. She's like all the rest of them.'

Flicka went down like a diver. She hit the ground with her legs folded under her, then rolled and bounced the rest of the way. It was exactly like the bronco that had climbed over the side of the truck and rolled down the forty-foot bank; and in silence the four watchers sat in their saddles waiting to see what would happen when she hit bottom – Ken already thinking of the Winchester, and the way the crack of it had echoed back from the hills.

Flicka lit, it seemed, on four steel springs that tossed her up and sent her flying down the mountainside – perfection of speed and power and action. A hot sweat bathed Ken from head to foot, and he began to laugh, half choking—

The wind roared down and swept up the fog, and it went bounding away over the hills, leaving trailing streamers of white in the gullies, and coverlets of cotton around the bushes. Way below, they could see Flicka galloping towards the yearlings. In a moment she joined them, and then there was just a many-coloured blur of moving shapes, with a fierce sun blazing down, striking sparks of light off their glossy coats.

'Get going!' shouted McLaughlin. 'Get around behind them. They're on the run now, and it's cleared – keep them running, and we may get them all in together, before they stop. Tim, you take the short way back to the gate and help Howard turn them and get them through.'

Tim shot off towards the County Road and the

other three riders galloped down and around the mountain until they were at the back of the band of yearlings. Shouting and yelling and spurring their mounts, they kept the colts running, circling them around towards the ranch until they had them on the County Road.

Way ahead, Ken could see Tim and Howard at the gate, blocking the road. The yearlings were bearing down on them. Now McLaughlin slowed up, and began to call, 'Whoa, whoa—' and the pace decreased. Often enough the yearlings had swept down that road and through the gate and down to the corrals. It was the pathway to oats, and hay, and shelter from winter storms – would they take it now? Flicka was with them – right in the middle – if they went, would she go too?

It was all over almost before Ken could draw a breath. The yearlings turned at the gate, swept through, went down to the corrals on a dead run, and through the gates that Gus had opened.

Flicka was caught again.

Mindful that she had clawed her way out when she was corralled before, McLaughlin determined to keep her in the main corral into which the stable door opened. It had eight-foot walls of aspen poles. The rest of the yearlings must be manoeuvred away from her.

Now that the fog had gone, the sun was scorching, and horses and men alike were soaked with sweat before the chasing was over and, one after the other, the yearlings had been driven into the other corral, and Flicka was alone.

She knew that her solitude meant danger, and that

she was singled out for some special disaster. She ran frantically to the high fence through which she could see the other ponies standing, and reared and clawed at the poles; she screamed, whirled, circled the corral first in one direction, and then the other. And while Mc-Laughlin and Ross were discussing the advisability of roping her, she suddenly espied the dark hole which was the open upper half of the stable door, and dived through it. McLaughlin rushed to close it, and she was caught – safely imprisoned in the stable.

The rest of the colts were driven away, and Ken stood outside the stable, listening to the wild hoofs beating, the screams, the crashes. His Flicka within there – close at hand – imprisoned. He was shaking. He felt a desperate desire to quiet her somehow, to *tell her*. If she only knew how he loved her, that there was nothing to be afraid of, that they were going to be friends—

Ross shook his head with a one-sided grin. 'Sure a wild one,' he said, coiling his lariat.

'Plumb loco,' said Tim briefly.

McLaughlin said, 'We'll leave her to think it over. After dinner we'll come up and feed and water her and do a little work with her.'

But when they went up after dinner there was no Flicka in the barn. One of the windows above the manger was broken, and the manger was full of pieces of glass.

Staring at it, McLaughlin gave a short laugh. He looked at Ken. 'She climbed into the manger – see? Stood on the feed box, beat the glass out with her front hoofs and climbed through.'

The window opened into the Six Foot Pasture. Near it was a wagon-load of hay. When they went around the back of the stable to see where she had gone they found her between the stable and the hay wagon, eating.

At their approach, she leaped away, then headed east across the pasture.

'If she's like her mother,' said Rob, 'she'll go right through the wire.'

'Ay bet she'll go over,' said Gus. 'She yumps like a deer.'

'No horse can jump that,' said McLaughlin.

Ken said nothing because he could not speak. It was the most terrible moment of his life. He watched Flicka racing towards the eastern wire.

A few rods from it, she swerved, turned and raced diagonally south.

'It turned her! It turned her!' cried Ken, almost sobbing. It was the first sign of hope for Flicka. 'Oh, Dad, she has got sense, she has! She has!'

Flicka turned again as she met the southern boundary of the pasture, again at the northern; she avoided the barn. Without abating anything of her whirlwind speed, following a precise, accurate calculation, and turning each time on a dime, she investigated every possibility. Then, seeing that there was no hope, she raced south towards the range where she had spent her life, gathered herself, and rose to the impossible leap.

Each of the men watching had the impulse to cover his eyes, and Ken gave a howl of despair.

Twenty yards of fence came down with her as she hurled herself through. Caught on the upper strands, she turned a complete somersault, landing on her back, her four legs dragging the wires down on top her, of and tangling herself in them beyond hope of escape.

'Damn the wire!' cursed McLaughlin. 'If I could afford decent fences—'

Ken followed the men miserably as they walked to the filly. They stood in a circle watching while she kicked and fought and thrashed until the wire was tightly wound and tangled about her, piercing and tearing her flesh and hide. At last she was unconscious, streams of blood running on her golden coat, and pools of crimson widening on the grass beneath her.

With the wire-cutters which Gus always carried in the hip pocket of his overalls, he cut the wire away; and they drew her into the pasture, repaired the fence, placed hay, a box of oats, and a tub of water near her, and called it a day.

'I doubt if she pulls out of it,' said McLaughlin briefly. 'But it's just as well. If it hadn't been this way it would have been another. A loco horse isn't worth a damn.'

Ken lay on the grass behind Flicka. One little brown hand was on her back, smoothing it, pressing softly, caressing. The other hand supported his head. His face hung over her.

His throat felt dry; his lips were like paper.

After a long while he whispered, 'I didn't mean to kill you, Flicka—'

Howard came to sit with him, quiet and respectful as is proper in the presence of grief or mourning.

'Gee! Highboy was never like that,' he said.

Ken made no answer to this. His eyes were on Flicka, watching her slow breathing. He had often seen horses down and unconscious. Badly cut with wire, too – they got well. Flicka could get well.

'Gosh! She's about as bad as Rocket,' said Howard cheerfully.

Ken raised his head scowling. 'Rocket! That old black hellion!'

'Well, Flicka's her child, isn't she?'

'She's Banner's child too—'

There were many air-tight compartments in Ken's mind. Rocket – now that she had come to a bad end – had conveniently gone into one of them.

After a moment Howard said, 'We haven't given our colts their workout today.' He pulled up his knees and clasped his hands around them.

Ken said nothing.

'We're supposed to, you know – we gotta,' said Howard. 'Dad'll be sore at us if we don't.'

'I don't want to leave her,' said Ken, and his voice was strange and thin.

Howard was sympathetically silent. Then he said, 'I could do your two for you, Ken—'

Ken looked up gratefully. 'Would you, Howard? Gee – that'd be keen—'

'Sure I'll do all of 'em, and you can stay here with Flicka.'

'Thanks.' Ken put his head down on his hand again, and the other hand smoothed and patted the filly's neck.

'Gee, she was pretty,' said Howard, sighing.

'What d'ya mean – *was*!' snapped Ken. 'You mean she *is* – she's beautiful.'

'I meant when she was running back there,' said Howard hastily.

Ken made no reply. It was true. Flicka floating across the ravines was something quite different from the inert mass lying on the ground, her belly rounded up into a mound, her neck weak and collapsed on the grass, her head stretched out, homely and senseless.

'Just think,' said Howard, 'you could have had any one of the other yearlings. And I guess by this time, it would been half tamed down there in the corral – probably tied to the post.'

As Ken still kept silent, Howard got slowly to his feet. 'Well, I guess I might as well go and do the colts,' he said, and walked away. At a little distance he turned. 'If Mother goes for the mail, do you want to go along?'

Ken shook his head.

When Howard was out of sight, Ken kneeled up and looked Flicka all over. He had never thought that, as soon as this, he would have been close enough to pat her, to caress her, to hold and examine her. He felt a passion of possession. Sick and half destroyed as she was, she was his own, and his heart was bursting with love of her. He smoothed her all over. He arranged her mane in more orderly fashion; he tried to straighten her head.

'You're mine now, Flicka,' he whispered.

He counted her wounds. The two worst were a deep cut above the right rear hock, and a long gash in her chest that ran down into the muscle of the foreleg.

Besides those, she was snagged with three-cornered tears through which the flesh pushed out, and laced with cuts and scratches with blood drying on them in rows of little black beads.

Ken wondered if the two bad cuts ought to be sewn up. He thought of Doc Hicks, and then remembered what his Dad had said: 'You cost me money every time you turn around.' No – Gus might do it – Gus was pretty good at sewing up animals. But Dad said best thing of all is usually to let them alone. They heal up. There was Sultan, hit by an automobile out on the highway; it knocked him down and took a big piece of flesh out of his chest and left the flap of skin hanging loose – and it all healed up of itself and you could only tell where the wound had been by the hair's being a different length.

The cut in Flicka's hind leg was awfully deep—

He put his head down against her and whispered again, 'Oh, Flicka – I didn't mean to kill you.'

After a few moments, 'Oh, get well – get well – *get well*—'

And again, 'Flicka, don't be so wild. *Be all right*, Flicka—'

Gus came out to him carrying a can of black grease.

'De Boss tole me to put some of dis grease on de filly's cuts, Ken – it helps heal 'em up.'

Together they went over her carefully, putting a smear of the grease wherever they could reach a wound.

Gus stood looking down at the boy.

'D'you think she'll get well, Gus?'

'She might, Ken. I seen plenty horses hurt as bad as

dot, and dey yust as good as ever.'

'Dad said—' But Ken's voice failed him when he remembered that his father had said she might as well die, because she was loco anyway.

The Swede stood a moment, his pale blue eyes, transparent and spiritual, looking kindly down at the boy; then he went on down to the barn.

Every trace of fog and mist had vanished, and the sun was blazing hot. Sweltering, Ken got up to take a drink of water from the bucket left for Flicka. Then, carrying handfuls of water in his small cupped hands, he poured it on her mouth. Flicka did not move, and once again Ken took his place behind her, his hand on her neck, his lips whispering to her.

After a while his head sank in exhaustion to the ground . . .

A roaring gale roused him and he looked up to see racing black clouds forming into a line. Blasts of cold wind struck down at the earth and sucked up leaves, twigs, tumbleweeds, in whorls like small cyclones.

From the black line in the sky, a fine icy mist sheeted down, and suddenly there came an appalling explosion of thunder. The world blazed and shuddered with lightning. High overhead was a noise like the shrieking of trumpets and trombones. The particles of fine icy mist beating down grew larger; they began to dance and bounce on the ground like little peas – like marbles – like ping-pong balls—

They beat upon Ken through his thin shirt and whipped his bare head and face. He kneeled up, leaning over Flicka, protecting her head with his folded arms. The hailstones were like ping-pong balls – like billiard balls – like little hard apples – like bigger apples – and suddenly, here and there, they fell as big as tennis balls, bouncing on the ground, rolling along, splitting on the rocks.

One hit Ken on the side of the face and a thin line of blood slid down his cheek with the water.

Running like a hare, under a pall of darkness, the storm fled eastwards, beating the grass flat upon the hills. Then, in the wake of the darkness and the screaming wind and hail, a clear silver light shone out, and the grass rose up again, every blade shimmering.

Watching Flicka, Ken sat back on his heels and sighed. She had not moved.

A rainbow, like a giant compass, drew a half circle of bright colour around the ranch. And off to one side, there was a vertical blur of fire hanging, left over from the storm.

Ken lay down again close behind Flicka and put his cheek against the soft tangle of her mane.

When evening came, and Nell had called Ken and had taken him by the hand and led him away, Flicka still lay without moving. Gently the darkness folded down over her. She was alone, except for the creatures of the sky – the heavenly bodies that wheeled over her; the two Bears, circling around the North Star; the cluster of little Sisters clinging together as if they held their arms wrapped around each other; the eagle, Aquila, that waited till nearly midnight before his great hidden wings lifted him above the horizon; and right overhead, an eye as bright as a blue diamond beaming down, the beautiful star, Vega.

Less alive than they, and dark under their brilliance,

the motionless body of Flicka lay on the blood-stained grass, earth-bound and fatal, every breath she drew a costly victory.

Towards morning, a half moon rode in the zenith.

A single, sharp, yapping bark broke the silence. Another answered, then another and another – tentative, questioning cries that presently became long quavering howls. The sharp pixie faces of a pack of coyotes pointed at the moon, and the howls trembled up through their long, tight-stretched throats and open, pulsating jaws. Each little prairie-wolf was allowed a solo, at first timid and wondering, then gathering force and impudence. Then they joined with each other and at last the troop was in full, yammering chorus, capering and malicious and thumbing noses and filling the air with sounds that raise the hair on human heads and put every animal on the alert.

Flicka came back to consciousness with a deep, shuddering sigh. She lifted her head and rolled over on her belly, drawing her legs under her a little. Resting so, she turned her head and listened. The yammer rose and fell. It was a familiar sound, she had heard it since she was born. The pack was across the stream on the edge of the woods beyond.

All at once, Flicka gathered herself, made a sudden, plunging effort, and gained her feet. It was not good for a filly to be helpless on the ground with a pack of coyotes near by. She stood swaying, her legs splayed out weakly, her head low and dizzy. It was minutes before balance came to her, and while she waited for it her nostrils flared, smelling water. *Water*! How near was it? Could she get to it?

She saw the tub and presently walked unsteadily over to it, put her lips in and drank. New life and strength poured into her. She paused, lifting her muzzle and mouthed the cold water, freshening her tongue and throat. She drank deeply again, then raised her head higher and stood with her neck turned, listening to the coyotes, until the sounds subsided, hesitated, died away.

She stood over the tub a long time. The pack yammered again, but the sound was like an echo, artless and hollow with distance, a mile away. They had gone across the valley for hunting.

A faint luminousness appeared over the earth and a lemon-coloured light in the east. One by one the stars drew back, and the pale, innocent blue of the early-morning sky closed over them.

By the time Ken reached Flicka in the morning, she had finished the water, eaten some of the oats, and was standing broadside to the level sunlight, gathering in every ultra-violet ray, every infra-red, for the healing and the recreation her battered body needed.

From *My Friend Flicka*

Bear

Alan Brownjohn

As a bear, I am
capable of so
much: running fast, smearing honey,
climbing trees – and an apparent slow
thoughtfulness.

It is hard then, that I should only want
to be bear-*like*: really, I
would swop it all, any day, to
live in Highgate as a bad-tempered old
grandfather-person, grumbling

(kindly) at children, sore-headed in
the garden, growling when the
tea is late, lumbering off
to play the piano in sulks in
a cold room in my heaviest overcoat.

From *Brownjohn's Beasts*

One of the most attractive of animals is the otter. In human terms they are happy, cheerful, full of fun, always ready for a rough and tumble – and they squeak with sheer joy. To have a companion like that about the house must make life very light and easy. BUT. And that's a very big but. They will chew your house to bits, they will attack your friends and they will bite the hand that feeds them if they are at all upset when things are not going their way. Terry Nutkin, who appears with me on *Animal Magic*, helped Gavin Maxwell, the author of the next story, to look after his otters. Terry understands otters very well, he knows how quick and vicious they can be; he is a most experienced handler of otters and yet he has been very severely bitten more than once. An otter can quite easily bite your finger right off – well, otters are very well equipped for chewing up large eels! You will learn in the story just how careful you have to be with otters.

Mijbil

Gavin Maxwell

I sit in a pitch-pine panelled kitchen–living room, with an otter asleep upon its back among the cushions on the sofa, forepaws in the air, and with the expression of tightly shut concentration that very small babies wear in sleep. Beyond the door is the sea, whose waves break on the beach no more than a stone's throw distant, and encircling, mist-hung mountains. A little group of Greylag geese sweep past the window and alight upon the small carpet of green turf; but for the soft, contented murmur of their voices and the sounds of the sea and the waterfall there is utter silence. This place has been my home now for ten years and more. It is also the home of two otters, Edal and Teko, and once it was the home of Mijbil, who first taught me what wonderful creatures otters are. The house is called Camusfeàrna, and it stands right at the edge of the sea in a wild and lonely part of the Scottish Highlands.

Mijbil's story begins a long way from Camusfeàrna, for he came from the great marshes of Southern Iraq, where the Tigris joins the Euphrates. A few years ago I travelled with Wilfred Thesiger, the explorer, to spend two months or so among the little-known Marsh Arabs, who live there. By then it had crossed my mind that I should like to keep an otter, and that

Camusfeàrna, ringed by water a stone's throw from its door, would be the right place for this experiment. I had mentioned this to Wilfred soon after the start of our journey, and he had replied that I had better get one in the Tigris marshes before I came home, for there they were as common as mosquitoes, and were often tamed by the Arabs.

We spent the better part of those two months squatting cross-legged in the bottom of a war canoe, travelling between the scattered reed-built villages; and at the end of our journey I did acquire an otter cub.

Wilfred Thesiger and I were both going to Basra, the nearest big town, to collect and answer our letters from home before setting off together again, but when we got there we found that Wilfred's mail had arrived but that mine had not, so I arranged to join Thesiger in a week's time, and he left without me.

Two days before the date of our rendezvous I returned to the Consulate-General, where I was living, late in the afternoon, having been out for several hours, to find my mail had arrived. I carried it to my bedroom to read, and there squatting on the floor were two Marsh Arabs; beside them lay a sack that squirmed from time to time.

They handed me a note from Wilfred. 'Here is your otter, a male and weaned. I feel you may want to take it to London – it would be a handful in the canoe.'

With the opening of that sack began a phase of my life that has not yet ended, and may, for all I know, not end before I do, because I can't any longer imagine being without an otter in the household.

The creature that emerged from this sack on to the spacious tiled floor of the Consulate bedroom, did not at that moment look like anything so much as a very small dragon. From the head to the tip of the tail it was coated with pointed scales of mud armour, between whose tips you could see a soft velvet fur like that of a chocolate-brown mole. He shook himself, and I half expected a cloud of dust, but the mud stayed where it was, and in fact it was not for another month that I managed to remove the last of it and see him, so to speak, in his true colours.

For the first twenty-four hours Mijbil was neither friendly nor unfriendly; he was simply aloof and indifferent, choosing to sleep on the floor as far from my bed as possible, and to accept food and water as though they were things that had appeared before him without human help. He ate small reddish fish from the Tigris, holding them upright between his forepaws, tail end uppermost, and eating them like a stick of Edinburgh rock, always with five crunches on the left-hand side of the jaw alternating with five crunches on the right.

The otter and I enjoyed the Consul-General's long-suffering hospitality for a fortnight. The second night Mijbil came to my bed in the small hours and remained asleep in the crook of my knees until the servant brought tea in the morning, and during that day he began to lose his sulks and take a keen, much too keen, interest in his surroundings. I made a collar, or rather a body-belt, for him, and took him on a lead to the bathroom, where for half an hour he went wild with joy in the water, plunging and rolling in it, shooting up and down the length of the bath underwater, and making enough slosh and splash for a hippo. This, I was to learn, is what otter do; every drop of water must be spread about the place; a bowl must at once be upset, or, if it will not overturn, be sat in and sploshed in until it overflows. Water must be kept on the move and made to do things.

It was only two days later that he escaped from my bedroom as I entered it, and I turned to see his tail disappearing round the bend of the corridor that led to the bathroom. By the time I had caught up with him he was up on the end of the bath and fumbling at the chromium taps with his paws. I watched, amazed; in less than a minute he had turned the tap far enough to produce a dribble of water, and, after a moment or two, the full flow. (He had, in fact, been lucky to turn the tap the right way; later he would as often as not try with great violence to screw it up still tighter, chittering with annoyance and disappointment at his failure.)

After a few days he would follow me without a lead and come to me when I called his name. By the end of a week he had accepted me completely and then he began to play. Very few species of animal play much after they are grown up, but otters are one of the exceptions to this rule; right through their lives they spend much of their time in play that does not even need a partner. In the wild state they will play alone for hours with some floating object in the water, pulling it down to let it bob up again, or throwing it with a jerk of the head so that it lands with a splash and becomes something to be chased. No doubt in their holts they lie on their backs and play too, as my otters have, with small objects that they can roll between their paws and pass from palm to palm, for at Camusfeàrna all the sea holts contain small shells and round stones that can only have been carried in for toys.

Mij would spend hours shuffling a rubber ball round the room like a four-footed soccer player, using all four feet to dribble the ball, and he could also throw it, with a powerful flick of the neck, to a surprising height and distance. These games he would play either by himself or with me, but the really steady play of an otter, the time-filling play born of a sense of well-being and a full stomach, seems to me to be when the otter lies on its back and juggles with small objects between its paws. Marbles became Mij's favourite toys for this pastime and he would lie on his back rolling two or more of them up and down his wide, flat belly without ever dropping one to the floor, or, with fore paws up-stretched, rolling them between his palms for minutes on end.

Even during that first fortnight in Basra I learnt a lot of Mij's language. The sounds are widely different in range. The simplest is the call note, which has been much the same in all the otters I have come across; it is a short, anxious mixture between a whistle and a chirp, and it can be heard for a long way. There is also a query, used at closer quarters; Mij would enter a room, for instance, and ask whether there was anyone in it by the word 'Ha!', in a loud, harsh whisper. But it was the chirp, high or low, from the single note to a con-tinuous flow of chitter, that was Mij's main means of talk.

An otter's jaws are, of course, very strong and those jaws have teeth meant to crunch into pulp fish heads that seem as hard as stone. Like a puppy that nibbles and gnaws one's hands because he has so few other outlets for his feelings, otters seem to find the use of

their mouths the most natural thing; knowing as I do their enormous crushing power I can see how hard my otters have tried to be gentle in play, but perhaps they think a human skin is as thick as an otter's. Mij used to look hurt and surprised when scolded for what must have seemed to him real gentleness, and though after a time he learned to be as soft-mouthed as a sucking dove with me, he remained all his life somewhat over-excitably good-humoured and hail-fellow-well-bit with strangers.

The days passed peacefully at Basra, but I dreaded the prospect of transporting Mij to England, and to Camusfeàrna. The air line insisted that Mij should be packed into a box of not more than eighteen inches square, and that this box must be personal luggage, to be carried on the floor at my feet.

The box was delivered on the afternoon before my departure on a 9.15 p.m. flight. It was zinc-lined and it seemed to me as nearly ideal as could be.

Dinner was at eight, and I thought that it would be as well to put Mij into the box an hour before we left, so that he would become accustomed to it before the jolting of the journey began to upset him. I got him into it, not without difficulty, and he seemed peaceful when I left him in the dark for a hurried meal.

But when I came back, with only barely time for the Consulate car to reach the airport for the flight, I saw an awful sight. There was complete silence from inside the box, but from its airholes and the chinks around the hinged lid, blood had trickled and dried on the white wood. I whipped off the padlock and tore open the lid, and Mij, exhausted and blood-spattered, whimpered and tried to climb up my leg. He had torn the zinc lining to shreds, scratching his mouth, his nose and his paws, and had left it jutting in spiky ribbons all around the walls and the floor of the box. When I had removed the last of it, so that there were no cutting edges left, it was just ten minutes until the time of the flight, and the airport was five miles distant. It was hard to bring myself to put the miserable Mij back into that box, that now seemed to him a torture chamber, but I forced myself to do it, slamming the lid down on my fingers as I closed it before he could make his escape. Then began a journey the like of which I hope I shall never know again.

I sat in the back of the car with the box beside me as the Arab driver tore through the streets of Basra like a bullet. Donkeys reared, bicycles swerved wildly, out in the suburbs goats stampeded and poultry found unguessed powers of flight. Mij cried unceasingly in the box, and both of us were hurled to and fro and up and down like drinks in a cocktail shaker. Exactly as we drew to a screeching stop before the airport entrance I heard a splintering sound from the box beside me, and saw Mij's nose force up the lid. He had summoned all the strength in his small body and torn one of the hinges clean out of the wood.

The aircraft was waiting to take off; as I was rushed through the customs by infuriated officials I was trying all the time to hold down the lid of the box with one hand, and with the other to force back the screws into the splintered wood.

It was perhaps my only stroke of fortune that the seat booked for me was at the extreme front of the aircraft, so that I had a bulkhead before me instead of another seat.

The port engines roared and then the starboard, and the aircraft trembled and teetered against the tug of her propellers, and then we were taxiing out to take off. Ten minutes later we were flying westwards over the great marshes that had been Mij's home, and peering downward into the dark I could see the glint of their waters beneath the moon.

I had brought a briefcase full of old newspapers, and a parcel of fish, and with these scant resources I prepared myself to withstand a siege.

I unlocked the padlock and opened the lid, and Mij was out like a flash. He dodged my fumbling hands with an eel-like wriggle and disappeared at high speed down the fuselage of the aircraft. As I tried to get into the gangway I could follow his progress among the passengers by a wave of disturbance among them not unlike that caused by the passage of a stoat through a hen run. There were squawks and shrieks and a flapping of travelling-coats, and halfway down the fuselage a woman stood up on her seat screaming out, 'A rat! A rat!'

I ran down the gangway and, catching sight of Mij's tail disappearing beneath the legs of a portly white-turbaned Indian, I tried a flying tackle, landing flat on my face. I missed Mij's tail, but found myself grasping the sandalled foot of the Indian's female companion; furthermore my face was inexplicably covered in curry. I staggered up babbling apology, and the Indian gave me a long silent stare, so blank that I could deduce from it no meaning whatsoever. I was, however, glad to see that something, possibly the curry, had won over the bulk of my fellow-passengers, and that they were regarding me now as a harmless clown rather than as a dangerous lunatic. The air hostess stepped into the breach.

'Perhaps,' she said with the most charming smile, 'it would be better if you resumed your seat, and I will find the animal and bring it to you.' I explained that Mij, being lost and frightened, might bite a stranger, but she did not think so. I returned to my seat.

I heard the ripple of flight and pursuit passing up and down the body of the aircraft behind me, but I could see little. I was craning my neck back over the seat trying to follow the hunt when suddenly I heard from my feet a distressed chitter of recognition and welcome, and Mij bounded on to my knee and began to nuzzle my face and neck. In all the strange world of the aircraft I was the only familiar thing to be found, and in that first return to me was sown the seed of the absolute trust that he gave me for the rest of his life.

Otters are extremely bad at doing nothing. That is to say that they cannot, as a dog does, lie still and awake; they are either asleep or entirely absorbed in play. If there is no toy, or if they are bored, they will set about laying the land waste. There is, I am convinced, something positively provoking to an otter about order and tidiness in any form, and the greater the untidiness that they can make the more contented they feel. A room does not seem right to them until they have turned everything upside down; cushions must be thrown to the floor from sofas and armchairs, books pulled out of bookcases, wastepaper baskets overturned and the rubbish spread as widely as possible, drawers opened and contents shovelled out and scattered. An otter must find out everything and have a hand in everything; but most of all he must know what lies inside any man-made container or beyond any man-made obstruction.

We had been flying for perhaps five hours when one of these moods descended upon Mijbil. It opened fairly harmlessly, with an attack upon the newspapers spread carefully round my feet, and in a minute or two the place looked like a street upon which royalty has been given a ticker-tape welcome. Then he turned his attentions to the box, where his sleeping compartment was filled with fine wood-shavings. First he put his head and shoulders in and began to throw these out backwards at enormous speed; then he got in bodily and lay on his back, using all four feet in a pedalling motion to hoist out the rest. I was doing my best to cope with the litter, but it was like a ship's pumps working against a leak too great for them, and I was hopelessly behind in the race when he turned his attention to my neighbour's canvas Trans-World travel bag on the floor beside him. The zipper gave him pause for no more than seconds; by chance, probably, he yanked it back and was in head first throwing out magazines, handkerchiefs, bottles of pills and tins of ear-plugs. By the grace of God my neighbour was asleep; I managed, unobserved, to haul Mij out by the tail and cram the things back somehow. I hoped that she might leave the aircraft at Cairo, before the outrage was discovered, and to my infinite relief she did so.

My troubles really began at Paris, a long time later. Mij had slept from time to time, but I had not closed an eye, and it was by now more than thirty-six hours since I had even dozed. I had to change airports, and, since I knew that Mij could slip his body strap with the least struggle, there was nothing else to do but put him back in his box. In its present form, however, the box was useless, for one hinge was dangling unattached from the lid.

I explained my predicament to the air hostess. She went forward to the crew's quarters, and returned after a few minutes saying that one of the crew would come and nail down the box and rope it for me. She warned me at the same time that Air France's rules differed from those of Trans-World, and that from Paris onward the box would have to travel freight and not in the passenger portion of the aircraft.

Mij was sleeping on his back inside my jacket, and I had to steel myself to betray his trust, to force him back into that hateful prison and listen to his pathetic cries as he was nailed in what now seemed to me like a coffin.

It was the small hours of the morning when we reached London Airport at last. I had cabled London and there was a hired car to meet me.

Mij, who had slept ever since the box was nailed up, was wide awake once more by the time we reached my flat; and when I had the driver paid off and the door closed behind me I prised open the lid of the box, and Mij clambered out into my arms to greet me with a frenzy of affection that I felt I had hardly deserved.

Otters that have been reared by human beings demand human company, much affection, and constant play; without these things they quickly become unhappy, and that makes them tiresome.

The spacious tile-floored bedroom of the Consulate-

General at Basra, with its minimum of furniture or bric-à-brac, had done little to prepare me for the problems that my crowded studio would present. Exhausted as he was that first night, Mij had not been out of his box for five minutes before he set out to explore his new quarters. I had gone to the kitchen to find fish for him, which I had arranged with my charlady to leave, but I had hardly got there before I heard the first crash of breaking china in the room behind me. The fish and the bath solved the problem for a while, for when he had eaten he went wild with joy in the water and romped for a full half hour, but it was clear that the flat would require a lot of alteration if it was to remain a home for both of us. Meanwhile sleep seemed long overdue, and I saw only one solution; I laid a sleeping-bag on the sofa, and anchored Mij to the sofa-leg by his lead.

Mij seemed to watch me closely as I composed myself on my back with a cushion under my head; then, with an air of knowing exactly what to do, he clambered up beside me and worked his body down into the sleeping-bag until he lay flat on his back inside it with his head on the cushion beside mine and his fore-paws in the air. In this position he heaved an enormous sigh and was instantly asleep.

Mij and I stayed in London for nearly a month, while, as my landlord put it, the studio came to look like a cross between a monkey-house and a furniture dump. A wire gate was fitted to the gallery stairs, so that he could sometimes be shut out of the studio itself; the upstairs telephone was enclosed in a box (whose fastening he early learned to undo); my dressing-table was cut off from him by a wire flap hinged from the ceiling, and the electric light wires were enclosed in tunnels of hardboard that made the place look like a powerhouse.

When he was loose in the studio, he would play for hours at a time with his favourite toys, ping-pong balls, marbles, indiarubber fruit and a terrapin shell that I had brought back from his native marshes. The smaller among these objects he could throw right across the room with a flick of his head, and with a ping-pong ball he invented a game of his own which would keep him happy for up to half an hour at a time. An expanding suitcase that I had taken to Iraq had become damaged on the journey home, so that the lid, when closed, remained at a slope from one end to the other. Mij discovered that if he put the ball on the high end it would run down the length of the suitcase unaided. He would dash round to the other end to ambush its arrival, hide from it, crouching, to spring up and take it by surprise as it reached the drop to the floor, grab it and trot off with it to the high end once more.

These games were enough for perhaps half of all the time he spent indoors and awake, but several times a day he needed a long romp with a human playmate. Tunnelling under the carpet and making believe that in doing so he became invisible, he would shoot out with a squeak of triumph if a foot passed within range; or he would dive inside the loose cover of the sofa and play tigers from behind it; or he would simply lay siege to one's person as a puppy does, bouncing around one in a frenzy of excited chirps and squeaks and launching a series of tip-and-run raids.

I soon found a way to distract his attention if he became too excitable. I would take the terrapin shell, wrap it in a towel, and knot the loose ends tightly across. He came to know these preparations, and would wait absolutely motionless until I handed him the bundle; then he would straddle it with his fore-arms, sink his teeth in the knots, and begin to hump and shuffle round the room. No matter how difficult the knots he would have them all undone in five or ten minutes, and then bring the towel and the terrapin shell to be tied up again. He brought the towel first, dragging it, and then made a second trip for the terrapin, shuffling it in front of him down the room like a football.

At night he slept in my bed, still, at this time, on his back with his head on the pillow, and in the morning he shared my bath. He would plunge ahead of me into water still too hot for me to enter, and while I shaved he would swim round me playing with the soapsuds or with celluloid and rubber ducks and ships.

Outside the house I took him for walks on a lead, just as if he had been a dog.

I was too timid of the result to allow him to meet any dog so to speak nose to nose, and I would pick him up if we met unattended dogs in the street, but for his part he seemed largely indifferent to them. The only time that I felt he knew that he had something in common with dogs was one morning when, setting out for his walk, he refused to be parted from a new toy, a large rubber ball painted in gaudy segments. This ball was too big for his mouth, so that he could only carry it sticking out from one side of his jaws like a gigantic gumboil, and thus burdened he set off briskly up the street, tugging at his lead. Rounding the first street corner we came face to face with a very fat spaniel, alone and carrying in his mouth a bundle of newspapers. The loads of the otter and the dog made it difficult for either of them to turn its head far as they came abreast, but their eyes rolled sideways with what appeared to me a wild surmise, and when they were a few paces past each other both suddenly stopped dead for a moment, as though each had suddenly realised something new.

It was not lack of curiosity, so much as lack of time and opportunity, that made me delay for nearly three weeks before making any real effort to find out Mij's race.

It is not, I suppose, in any way strange that most Londoners should not recognise an otter. Otters belong to a small group of animals called Mustellines, shared by the badger, mongoose, weasel, stoat, polecat, marten, mink and others. In the London streets, I faced continual questions that mentioned all the Mustellines but the otter; wilder, more random fire hit on practically everything from 'a baby seal' to a squirrel. The seal idea had deep root, and was perhaps the commonest of them all, though far from being the most odd. 'Is that a walrus, mister?' reduced me to giggles outside Harrods, and 'a hippo' made my day outside Cruft's Dog Show. A beaver, a bear cub, a newt, a leopard – one, apparently, that had changed his spots – even a 'brontosaur'; Mij was anything but an otter.

At last I telephoned to the Natural History department of the British Museum, in Cromwell Road, and the same afternoon Mr Robert Hayman arrived at my flat to examine two skins I had bought in Iraq and the living Mijbil, and in due course, Mij's new race was proclaimed. Hayman summoned me to the Museum to see the cabinets of otter skins from all over Asia, where the larger of mine lay, unlabelled and quite different from any other, in a drawer by itself, but beside its nearest relatives. These were of a variety of hues from pale sandy to medium brown, but none had been recorded west of Sind, in India, and none resembled mine in colour.

There are very few people who stumble upon a sizeable mammal previously unknown to science; in the nursery world of picture-books of birds and beasts the few who had given their own names to species – Steller's Eider and Sea Eagle, Sharpe's Crow, Humboldt's Woolly Monkey, Meinertzhagen's Forest Hog, Ross's Snow Goose, Grant's Gazelle, Père David's Deer – had been something like gods to me; they seemed like creators. Now, when Hayman suggested that the new otter should bear my name, something small and shrill from the nursery days was shouting inside me that I could become one of these gods and wear the halo of a creator. 'Can I have it for my own?' we used to ask when we were small. 'For my *very* own?' Here, surely, was an animal of my very own, to bear my name; every animal that looked like it would always bear my name for ever and ever.

So Mij and all his race became *Lutrogale perspicillata maxwelli*, and though he is now no more, and there is no real proof that there is another of his kind living in the world, I had got where I once wanted to be, and there was a Maxwell's otter.

From *The Otter's Tale*

The great thing about parrots is not so much what they say but when they say it. Parrots have wonderful timing. They choose just the right moment to say their little piece or make their favourite noise. I once bought an African Grey parrot in a pet shop. It was during the war and London was getting bombed pretty well every night. The pet shop was in Camden Town and as far as I remember this parrot was about the only animal in the place. I bought him and took him back to the farm in the country. He didn't say a word for months and I thought that he must have been severely disturbed by the constant bombing he had put up with, because the only noise he made was the terrifying noise of a bomb whistling down. He did it perfectly. WHHHHHHeeeeeeeEEEEEEE. And then he made a great CLICK, the best he could do for the bursting of a bomb.

His name was Plonky. I would sometimes say to him 'Send a bomb down, Plonky.' And Plonky would do his spectacular descending whistle, a perfect imitation of a falling bomb. But he would also do it when

I *hadn't* ask him to send a bomb down. Sometimes friends used to come down from London to spend the weekend and get a bit of peace from the bombing. Plonky would wait quietly, just watching us finish dinner. He would choose the exact moment when the conversation had died down, and then send a giant bomb down. WHHHHHHeeeeeeeEEEEEEE. You should have seen our guests dive under the table! You should have heard Plonky's dirty throaty laugh. Parrots are like that.

Parrot

Alan Brownjohn

Sometimes I sit with both eyes closed,
But all the same, I've heard!
They're saying, 'He won't talk because
He is a *thinking* bird.'

I'm olive-green and sulky, and
The family say, 'Oh yes,
He's silent, but he's *listening*,
He *thinks* more than he *says*!

'He ponders on the things he hears,
Preferring not to chatter.'
– And this is true, but *why* it's true
Is quite another matter.

I'm working out some shocking things
In order to surprise them,
And when my thoughts are ready I'll
Certainly *not* disguise them!

I'll wait, and see, and choose a time
When everyone is present,
And clear my throat and raise my beak
And give a squawk and start to speak
And go on for about a week
And it will not be pleasant!

From *Brownjohn's Beasts*

I suppose there are more stories about dogs than about any other animals. I know that people talk about their dogs a great deal. You've heard them. 'No, he *won't* touch chocolate cake or anything with any coconut in it, but *fruit* cake, now he *loves* a bit of fruit cake.' 'Yes, well our Tinker loves crisps, all I've got to do is go to the cupboard and say "Crisps, Tinker," you know, and he sits with his head on one side, he knows you know, and then I throw him the packet. He can open that packet in a flash and he'll eat the lot!'

'Have you seen him do that trick with the eggs?' Someone once said that to me and I answered, 'No, what trick with the eggs?' 'I'll get a couple of eggs.' I was staying in a small hotel and the owner had a strange mongrel dog with a most sad face. I was sitting in the lounge and a waiter was serving tea. He was only interested in serving tea and no doubt had seen this dog do the egg trick many times. The owner came back with two eggs and put them on the carpet in the middle of the lounge. The sad-faced dog knew exactly what was expected of him. He walked slowly up to the eggs and sat down. And then with his sharp inscisor tooth he made a small hole in each egg and sucked each one dry, leaving the shells absolutely intact. He had just finished the last egg when the waiter came in with a tray of tea and trod firmly on the two egg-shells.

There was an awful crunch. We were all just about to applaud the sad-faced dog for his trick when that waiter's great hoof absolutely destroyed his act. I have never seen such an expression on a dog's face. He looked up at the waiter and, there was no doubt about it, he said, 'You clumsy great oaf.'

As I say, there are many stories about dogs. Of their intelligence, their devotion and their bravery. The story of White Fang is very famous and it is very well observed. I have chosen an extract that shows how you gain the confidence of an animal.

White Fang

Jack London

'It's hopeless,' Weedon Scott confessed.

He sat on the step of his cabin and stared at the dog-musher, who responded with a shrug that was equally hopeless.

Together they looked at White Fang at the end of his stretched chain, bristling, snarling, ferocious, straining to get at the sled-dogs. Having received sundry lessons from Matt, said lessons being imparted by means of a club, the sled-dogs had learned to leave White Fang alone.

'It's a wolf and there's no taming it,' Weedon Scott announced.

'Oh, I don't know about that,' Matt objected. 'Might be a lot of dog in 'im for all you can tell. But there's one thing I know sure, an' that there's no gettin' away from.' The dog-musher indicated White Fang with a backward thrust of his thumb. 'Wolf or dog, it's all the same – he's ben tamed a'ready.'

'No!'

'I tell you yes, an' broke to harness. Look close there. D'ye see them marks across the chest?'

'You're right, Matt. He was a sled-dog before Beauty Smith got hold of him.'

'An' there's not much reason against his bein' a sled-dog again.'

'What d'ye think?' Scott queried eagerly. Then the hope died down as he added, shaking his head. 'We've had him two weeks now, and if anything, he's wilder than ever at the present moment.'

'Give 'm a chance,' Matt counselled. 'Turn 'm loose for a spell.'

The other looked at him incredulously.

'Yes,' Matt went on, 'I know you've tried to, but you didn't take a club.'

'You try it then.'

The dog-musher secured a club and went over to the chained animal. White Fang watched the club after the manner of a caged lion watching the whip of its trainer.

'See 'm keep his eye on that club,' Matt said. 'That's a good sign. He's no fool. Don't dast tackle me so long as I got that club handy. He's not clean crazy, sure.'

As the man's hand approached his neck, White Fang bristled and snarled and crouched down. But while he eyed the approaching hand, he at the same time contrived to keep track of the club in the other hand, suspended threateningly above him. Matt unsnapped the chain from the collar and stepped back.

White Fang could scarcely realise that he was free. Many months had gone by since he passed into the possession of Beauty Smith, and in all that period he had never known a moment of freedom except at the times he had been loosed to fight with other dogs. Immediately after such fights he had been imprisoned again.

He did not know what to make of it. Perhaps some new deviltry of the gods was about to be perpetrated on him. He walked slowly and cautiously, prepared to be assailed at any moment. He did not know what to do, it was all so unprecedented. He took the precaution to sheer off from the two watching gods, and walked carefully to the corner of the cabin. Nothing happened. He was plainly perplexed, and he came back again, pausing a dozen feet away and regarding the two men intently.

'Won't he run away?' his new owner asked.

Matt shrugged his shoulders. 'Got to take a gamble. Only way to find out is to find out.'

'Poor devil,' Scott murmured pityingly. 'What he needs is some show of human kindness,' he added, turning and going into the cabin.

He came out with a piece of meat, which he tossed to White Fang. He sprang away from it, and from a distance studied it suspiciously.

'Hi-yu, Major!' Matt shouted warningly, but too late.

Major had made a spring for the meat. At the instant his jaws closed on it, White Fang struck him. He was overthrown. Matt rushed in, but quicker than he was White Fang. Major staggered to his feet, but the blood spouting from his throat reddened the snow in a widening path.

'It's too bad, but it served him right,' Scott said hastily.

But Matt's foot had already started on its way to kick White Fang. There was a leap, a flash of teeth, a sharp exclamation. White Fang, snarling fiercely, scrambled backward for several yards, while Matt stooped and investigated his leg.

'He got me all right,' he announced, pointing to the torn trousers and underclothes, and the growing stain of red.

'I told you it was hopeless, Matt,' Scott said in a dis-
couraged voice. 'I've thought about it off and on,
while not wanting to think of it. But we've come to it
now. It's the only thing to do.'

As he talked, with reluctant movements he drew his
revolver, threw open the cylinder, and assured himself
of its contents.

'Look here, Mr Scott,' Matt objected; 'that dog's
ben through hell. You can't expect 'm to come out a
white an' shining angel. Give 'm time.'

'Look at Major,' the other rejoined.

The dog-musher surveyed the stricken dog. He had
sunk down on the snow in the circle of his blood, and
was plainly in the last gasp.

'Served 'm right. You said so yourself, Mr Scott. He
tried to take White Fang's meat, an' he's dead-O. That
was to be expected. I wouldn't give two whoops in
hell for a dog that wouldn't fight for his own meat.'

'But look at yourself, Matt. It's all right about the
dogs, but we must draw the line somewhere.'

'Served me right,' Matt argued stubbornly. 'What'd
I want to kick 'm for? You said yourself he'd done
right. Then I had no right to kick 'm.'

'It would be a mercy to kill him,' Scott insisted. He's
untameable.'

'Now look here, Mr Scott, give the poor devil a
fightin' chance. He ain't had no chance yet. He's just
come through hell, an' this is the first time he's ben
loose. Give 'm a fair chance, an' if he don't deliver the
goods, I'll kill 'm myself. There!'

'God knows I don't want to kill him or have him
killed,' Scott answered, putting away the revolver.
'We'll let him run loose and see what kindness can do

for him. And here's a try at it.' He walked over to White Fang and began talking to him gently and soothingly.

'Better have a club handy,' Matt warned.

Scott shook his head and went on trying to win White Fang's confidence. White Fang was suspicious. Something was impending. He had killed this god's dog, bitten his companion god, and what else was to be expected than some terrible punishment? But in the face of it he was indomitable. He bristled and showed his teeth, his eyes vigilant, his whole body wary and prepared for anything. The god had no club, so he suffered him to approach quite near. The god's hand had come out and was descending on his head. White Fang shrank together and grew tense as he crouched under it. Here was danger, some treachery or something. He knew the hands of the gods, their proved mastery, their cunning to hurt. Besides, there was his old antipathy to being touched. He snarled more menacingly, crouched still lower, and still the hand descended. He did not want to bite the hand, and he endured the peril of it until his instinct surged up in him, mastering him with its insatiable yearning for life.

Weedon Scott had believed that he was quick enough to avoid any snap or slash. But he had yet to learn the remarkable quickness of White Fang, who struck with the certainty and swiftness of a coiled snake.

Scott cried out sharply with surprise, catching his torn hand and holding it tightly in his other hand. Matt uttered a great oath and sprang to his side. White Fang crouched down and backed away, bristling, showing his fangs, his eyes malignant with menace.

Now he could expect a beating as fearful as any he had received from Beauty Smith.

'Here! What are you doing?' Scott cried suddenly.

Matt had dashed into the cabin and come out with a rifle.

'Nothin',' he said slowly, with a careless calmness that was assumed; 'only goin' to keep that promise I made. I reckon it's up to me to kill 'm as I said I'd do.'

'No you don't!'

'Yes I do. Watch me.'

As Matt had pleaded for White Fang when he had been bitten, it was now Weedon Scott's turn to plead.

'You said to give him a chance. Well, give it to him. We've only just started, and we can't quit at the beginning. It served me right, this time. And – look at him!'

White Fang, near the corner of the cabin and forty feet away, was snarling with blood-curdling viciousness, not at Scott, but at the dog-musher.

'Well, I'll be everlastin'ly gosh-swoggled!' was the dog-musher's expression of astonishment.

'Look at the intelligence of him,' Scott went on hastily. 'He knows the meaning of firearms as well as you do. He's got intelligence, and we've got to give that intelligence a chance. Put up that gun.'

'All right, I'm willin',' Matt agreed, leaning the rifle against the woodpile.

'But will you look at that!' he exclaimed the next moment.

White Fang had quieted down and ceased snarling.

'This is worth investigatin'. Watch.'

Matt reached for the rifle, and at the same moment White Fang snarled. He stepped away from the rifle, and White Fang's lifted lips descended, covering his teeth.

Matt took the rifle and began slowly to raise it to his shoulder. White Fang's snarling began with the movement, and increased as the movement approached its culmination. But the moment before the rifle came to a level with him, he leaped sidewise behind the corner of the cabin. Matt stood staring along the sights at the empty space of snow which had been occupied by White Fang.

The dog-musher put the rifle down solemnly, then turned and looked at his employer.

'I agree with you, Mr Scott. That dog's too intelligent to kill.'

As White Fang watched Weedon Scott approach, he bristled and snarled to advertise that he would not submit to punishment. Twenty-four hours had passed since he had slashed open the hand that was now bandaged and held up by a sling to keep the blood out of it. In the past White Fang had experienced delayed punishments, and he apprehended that such a one was about to befall him. How could it be otherwise? He had committed what was to him sacrilege, sunk his fangs in the holy flesh of a god, and of a white-skinned superior god at that. In the nature of things, and of intercourse with gods, something terrible awaited him.

The god sat down several feet away. White Fang could see nothing dangerous in that. When the gods administered punishment they stood on their legs. Besides, this god had no club, no whip, no firearm. And furthermore, he himself was free. No chain nor stick bound him. He could escape into safety while the god scrambled to his feet. In the meantime he would wait and see.

The god remained quiet, made no movement; and White Fang's snarl slowly dwindled to a growl that ebbed down in his throat and ceased. Then the god spoke, and at the first sound of his voice, the hair rose on White Fang's neck and the growl rushed up in his throat. But the god made no hostile movement and went on calmly talking. For a time White Fang growled in unison with him, a correspondence of rhythm being established between growl and voice. But the god talked on interminably. He talked to White Fang as White Fang had never been talked to before. He talked softly and soothingly with a gentleness that somehow, somewhere, touched White Fang, In spite of himself and all the pricking warnings of his instinct, White Fang began to have confidence in this god.

After a long time, the god got up and went into the cabin. White Fang scanned him apprehensively when he came out. He had neither whip nor club nor weapon. Nor was his injured hand behind his back hiding something. He sat down as before, in the same spot, several feet away. He held out a small piece of meat. White Fang pricked up his ears and investigated it suspiciously, managing to look at the same time both at the meat and the god, his body tense and ready to spring away at the first sign of hostility.

Still the punishment delayed. The god merely held near to his nose a piece of meat. And about the meat there seemed nothing wrong. Still White Fang suspected; and though the meat was proffered to him with short inviting thrusts of the hand, he refused to touch it. In past experience, especially in dealing with squaws, meat and punishment had often been disastrously related.

In the end, the god tossed the meat on the snow at White Fang's feet. He smelled the meat carefully; but he did not look at it. While he smelled it he kept his eyes on the god. Nothing happened. He took the meat into his mouth and swallowed it. Still nothing happened. The god was actually offering him another piece of meat. Again he refused to take it from the hand, and again it was tossed to him. This was repeated a number of times. But there came a time when the god refused to toss it. He kept it in his hand and steadfastly proffered it.

The meat was good meat, and White Fang was hungry. Bit by bit, infinitely cautious, he approached the hand. At last the time came that he decided to eat the meat from the hand. He never took his eyes from the god, thrusting his head forward with ears flattened back and hair involuntarily rising and crested on his neck. Also a low growl rumbled in his throat as warning that he was not to be trifled with. He ate the meat, and nothing happened. Piece by piece, he ate all the meat, and nothing happened.

He licked his chops and waited. The god went on talking. In his voice was kindness – something of which White Fang had no experience whatever. And within him it aroused feelings which he had likewise never experienced before. He was aware of a certain strange satisfaction, as though some need were being gratified, as though some void in his being were being filled.

Ah, he had thought so! There it came now, the god's

hand, cunning to hurt, thrusting out at him, descending upon his head. But the god went on talking. His voice was soft and soothing. In spite of the menacing hand, the voice inspired confidence. And in spite of the assuring voice, the hand inspired distrust. White Fang was torn by conflicting feelings, impulses.

The hand lifted and descended again in a patting, caressing movement. This continued, but every time the hand lifted the hair lifted under it. And every time the hand descended, the ears flattened down and a cavernous growl surged in his throat. White Fang growled with insistent warning. By this means he announced that he was prepared to retaliate for any hurt he might receive.

But the god talked on softly, and ever the hand rose and fell with non-hostile pats. White Fang expressed dual feelings. It was distasteful to his instinct. It restrained him, opposed the will of him toward personal liberty. And yet it was not physically painful. On the contrary, it was even pleasant, in a physical way. The patting movement slowly and carefully changed to a rubbing of the ears about their bases; the physical pleasure increased a little.

'Well, I'll be gosh-swoggled!'

So spoke Matt, coming out of the cabin, his sleeves rolled up, a pan of dirty dish-water in his hands, arrested in the act of emptying the pan by the sight of Weedon Scott patting White Fang.

At the instant his voice broke the silence, White Fang leaped back, snarling savagely at him.

Matt regarded his employer with grieved disapproval.

'If you don't mind my expressin' my feelin's, Mr Scott, I'll make free to say you're seventeen kinds of a damn fool an' all of 'em different, and then some.'

Weedon Scott smiled with a superior air, gained his feet and walked over to White Fang. He talked soothingly to him, but not for long, then slowly put out his hand, rested it on White Fang's head, and resumed the interrupted patting. White Fang endured it, keeping his eyes fixed suspiciously, not upon the man that patted him, but upon the man that stood in the doorway.

'You may be a number one, tip-top minin' expert, all right all right,' the dog-musher delivered himself oracularly, 'but you missed the chance of your life when you was a boy an' didn't run off an' join a circus.'

From *White Fang*

Zoo Manners

Eileen Mathias

Be careful what
   You say or do
When you visit the animals
   At the Zoo.

Don't make fun
   Of the Camel's hump –
He's very proud
   Of his noble bump.

Don't laugh too much
   At the Chimpanzee –
He think's he's as wise
   As you or me.

And the Penguins
   Strutting round the lake
Can understand
   Remarks you make.

Treat them as well
   As they do you,
And you'll always be welcome
   At the Zoo.

From *Come Follow Me*

The Big Baboon

Hilaire Belloc

The Big Baboon is found upon
  The plains of Cariboo:
He goes about with nothing on
  (A shocking thing to do).

But if he dressed respectably
  And let his whiskers grow,
How like this Big Baboon would be
  To Mister So-and-so!

From *The Complete Verse of Hilaire Belloc*

I like the *Just So Stories* very much and have read some
of them on *Animal Magic*. This is one of my favourites
and is a good one to read aloud, particularly the bit
about the 'great grey-green, greasy Limpopo River!'
Like all children the Elephant's Child is always asking
questions and nearly gets more than he bargained for!

The Elephant's Child

Rudyard Kipling

In the High and Far-Off Times the Elephant, O Best Beloved, had no trunk. He had only a blackish, bulgy nose, as big as a boot, that he could wriggle about from side to side; but he couldn't pick up things with it. But there was one Elephant – a new Elephant – an Elephant's Child – who was full of 'satiable curtiosity, and that means he asked ever so many questions. *And* he lived in Africa, and he filled all Africa with his 'satiable curtiosities. He asked his tall aunt, the Ostrich, why her tail-feathers grew just so, and his tall aunt the Ostrich spanked him with her hard, hard claw. He asked his tall uncle, the Giraffe, what made his skin spotty, and his tall uncle, the Giraffe, spanked him with his hard, hard hoof. And still he was full of 'satiable curtiosity! He asked his broad aunt, the Hippopotamus, why her eyes were red, and his broad aunt, the Hippopotamus, spanked him with her broad, broad hoof; and he asked his hairy uncle, the Baboon, why melons tasted just so, and his hairy uncle, the Baboon, spanked him with his hairy, hairy paw. And *still* he was full of 'satiable curtiosity! He asked questions about everything that he saw, or heard, or felt, or smelt, or touched, and all his uncles and his aunts spanked him. And still he was full of 'satiable curtiosity!

One fine morning in the middle of the Precession of the Equinoxes this 'satiable Elephant's Child asked a new fine question that he had never asked before. He asked, 'What does the Crocodile have for dinner?' Then everybody said, 'Hush!' in a loud and dretful tone, and they spanked him immediately and directly, without stopping, for a long time.

By and by, when that was finished, he came upon Kolokolo Bird sitting in the middle of a wait-a-bit thorn-bush, and he said, 'My father has spanked me, and my mother has spanked me; all my aunts and uncles have spanked me for my 'satiable curtiosity; and *still* I want to know what the Crocodile has for dinner!'

Then Kolokolo Bird said, with a mournful cry, 'Go to the banks of the great grey-green, greasy Limpopo River, all set about with fever-trees, and find out.'

That very next morning, when there was nothing left of the Equinoxes, because the Precession had preceded according to precedent, this 'satiable Elephant's Child took a hundred pounds of bananas (the little short red kind), and a hundred pounds of sugar-cane (the long purple kind), and seventeen melons (the greeny-crackly kind), and said to all his dear families, 'Goodbye. I am going to the great grey-green, greasy Limpopo River, all set about with fever-trees, to find out what the Crocodile has for dinner.' And they all spanked him once more for luck, though he asked them most politely to stop.

Then he went away, a little warm, but not at all astonished, eating melons, and throwing the rind about, because he could not pick it up.

He went from Graham's Town to Kimberley, and from Kimberley to Khama's Country, and from Khama's Country he went east by north, eating melons all the time, till at last he came to the banks of the great grey-green, greasy Limpopo River, all set about with fever-trees, precisely as Kolokolo Bird had said.

Now you must know and understand, O Best Beloved, that till that very week, and day, and hour, and minute, this 'satiable Elephant's Child had never seen a Crocodile, and did not know what one was like. It was all his 'satiable curtiosity.

The first thing that he found was a Bi-Coloured-Python-Rock-Snake curled round a rock.

' 'Scuse me,' said the Elephant Child's most politely, 'but have you seen such a thing as a Crocodile in these promiscuous parts?'

'*Have* I seen a Crocodile?' said the Bi-Coloured-Python-Rock-Snake, in a voice of dretful scorn. 'What will you ask me next?'

' 'Scuse me,' said the Elephant's Child, 'but could you kindly tell me what he has for dinner?'

Then the Bi-Coloured-Python-Rock-Snake uncoiled himself very quickly from the rock and spanked the Elephant's Child with his scalesome, flailsome tail.

'That is odd,' said the Elephant's Child, 'because my father and my mother, and my uncle and my aunt, not to mention my other aunt, the Hippopotamus, and my other uncle, the Baboon, have all spanked me for my 'satiable curtiosity – and I suppose this is the same thing.'

So he said good-bye very politely to the Bi-Coloured-Python-Rock-Snake, and helped to coil him up on the rock again, and went on, a little warm, but not at all astonished, eating melons, and throwing the rind about, because he could not pick it up, till he trod on what he thought was a log of wood at the very edge of the great grey-green, greasy Limpopo River, all set about with fever-trees.

But it was really the Crocodile, O Best Beloved, and the Crocodile winked one eye – like this!

' 'Scuse me,' said the Elephant's Child most politely, 'but do you happen to have seen a Crocodile in these promiscuous parts?'

Then the Crocodile winked the other eye, and lifted half his tail out of the mud; and the Elephant's Child stepped back most politely, because he did not wish to be spanked again.

'Come hither, Little One,' said the Crocodile. 'Why do you ask such things?'

' 'Scuse me,' said the Elephant's Child most politely, 'but my father has spanked me, my mother has spanked me, not to mention my tall aunt, the Ostrich, and my tall uncle, the Giraffe, who can kick ever so hard, as well as my broad aunt, the Hippopotamus, and my hairy uncle, the Baboon, *and* including the Bi-Coloured-Python-Rock-Snake, with the scalesome, flailsome tail, just up the bank, who spanks harder than any of them; and *so*, if it's quite all the same to you, I don't want to be spanked any more.'

'Come hither, Little One,' said the Crocodile, 'for I am the Crocodile,' and he wept crocodile-tears to show it was quite true.

Then the Elephant's Child grew all breathless, and panted, and kneeled down on the bank and said, 'You are the very person I have been looking for all these long days. Will you please tell me what you have for dinner?'

'Come hither, Little One,' said the Crocodile, 'and I'll whisper.'

Then the Elephant's Child put his head down close to the Crocodile's musky, tusky mouth, and the Crocodile caught him by his little nose, which up to that very week, day, hour, and minute, had been no bigger than a boot, though much more useful.

'I think,' said the Crocodile – and he said it between his teeth, like this – 'I think to-day I will begin with Elephant's Child!'

At this, O Best Beloved, the Elephant's Child was much annoyed, and he said, speaking through his nose, like this, 'Led go! You are hurtig be!'

Then the Bi-Coloured-Python-Rock-Snake scuffled down from the bank and said, 'My young friend, if you do not now, immediately and instantly, pull as hard as ever you can, it is my opinion that your acquaintance in the large-pattern leather ulster' (and by this he meant the Crocodile) 'will jerk you into yonder limpid stream before you can say Jack Robinson.'

This is the way Bi-Coloured-Python-Rock-Snakes always talk.

Then the Elephant's Child sat back on his little haunches, and pulled, and pulled, and pulled, and his nose began to stretch. And the Crocodile floundered into the water, making it all creamy with great sweeps of his tail, and *he* pulled, and pulled, and pulled.

And the Elephant's Child's nose kept on stretching; and the Elephant's Child spread all his little four legs and pulled, and pulled, and pulled, and his nose kept on stretching; and the Crocodile threshed his tail like an oar, and *he* pulled, and pulled, and pulled, and at each pull the Elephant's Child's nose grew longer and longer – and it hurt him hijjus!

Then the Elephant's Child felt his legs slipping, and he said through his nose, which was now nearly five feet long, 'This so too buch for be!'

Then the Bi-Coloured-Python-Rock-Snake came down from the bank, and knotted himself in a double-clove-hitch round the Elephant's Child's hind-legs, and said, 'Rash and inexperienced traveller, we will now seriously devote ourselves to a little high tension, because if we do not, it is my impression that yonder self-propelling man-of-war with the armour-plated upper deck' (and by this, O Best Beloved, he meant the Crocodile) 'will permanently vitiate your future career.'

That is the way all Bi-Coloured-Python-Rock-Snakes always talk.

So he pulled, and the Elephant's Child pulled, and the Crocodile pulled; but the Elephant's Child and the Bi-Coloured-Python-Rock-Snake pulled hardest; and at last the Crocodile let go of the Elephant's Child's nose with a plop that you could hear all up and down the Limpopo.

Then the Elephant's Child sat down most hard and sudden; but first he was careful to say 'Thank you' to the Bi-Coloured-Python-Rock-Snake; and next he was kind to his poor pulled nose, and wrapped it all up in cool banana leaves, and hung it in the great grey-green, greasy Limpopo to cool.

'What are you doing that for?' said the Bi-Coloured-Python-Rock-Snake.

' 'Scuse me,' said the Elephant's Child, 'but my nose is badly out of shape, and I am waiting for it to shrink.'

'Then you will have to wait a long time,' said the Bi-Coloured-Python-Rock-Snake. 'Some people do not know what is good for them.'

The Elephant's Child sat there for three days waiting for his nose to shrink. But it never grew any shorter, and, besides, it made him squint. For, O Best Beloved, you will see and understand that the Crocodile had pulled it out into a really truly trunk same as all Elephants have to-day.

At the end of the third day a fly came and stung him on the shoulder, and before he knew what he was doing he lifted up his trunk and hit that fly dead with the end of it.

' 'Vantage number one!' said the Bi-Coloured-Python-Rock-Snake. 'You couldn't have done that with a mere-smear nose. Try and eat a little now.'

Before he thought what he was doing the Elephant's Child put out his trunk and plucked a large bundle of grass, dusted it clean against his fore-legs, and stuffed it into his own mouth.

' 'Vantage number two!' said the Bi-Coloured-Python-Rock-Snake. 'You couldn't have done that with a mere-smear nose. Don't you think the sun is very hot here?'

'It is,' said the Elephant's Child, and before he thought what he was doing he schlooped up a schloop of mud from the banks of the great grey-green, greasy Limpopo, and slapped it on his head, where it made a cool schloopy-sloshy mud-cap all trickly behind his ears.

' 'Vantage number three!' said the Bi-Coloured-Python-Rock-Snake. 'You couldn't have done that with a mere-smear nose. Now how do you feel about being spanked again?'

' 'Scuse me,' said the Elephant's Child, 'but I should not like it at all.'

'How would you like to spank somebody?' said the Bi-Coloured-Python-Rock-Snake.

'I should like it very much indeed,' said the Elephant's Child.

'Well,' said the Bi-Coloured-Python-Rock-Snake, 'you will find that new nose of yours very useful to spank people with.'

'Thank you,' said the Elephant's Child. 'I'll remember that; and now I think I'll go home to all my dear families and try.'

So the Elephant's Child went home across Africa frisking and whisking his trunk. When he wanted fruit to eat he pulled fruit down from a tree, instead of waiting for it to fall as he used to do. When he wanted grass he plucked grass up from the ground, instead of going on his knees as he used to do. When the flies bit him he broke off the branch of a tree and used it as a fly-whisk; and he made himself a new, cool, slushy-squshy mud-cap whenever the sun was hot. When he felt lonely walking through Africa he sang to himself down his trunk, and the noise was louder than several brass bands. He went specially out of his way to find a broad Hippopotamus (she was no relation of his), and he spanked her very hard, to make sure that the Bi-Coloured-Python-Rock-Snake had spoken the truth about his new trunk. The rest of the time he picked up the melon-rinds that he had dropped on his way to the Limpopo – for he was a Tidy Pachyderm.

One dark evening he came back to all his dear families, and he coiled up his trunk and said, 'How do you do?' They were very glad to see him, and immediately said, 'Come here and be spanked for your 'satiable curtiosity.'

'Pooh,' said the Elephant's Child. 'I don't think you peoples know anything about spanking; but *I* do, and I'll show you.'

Then he uncurled his trunk and knocked two of his dear brothers head over heels.

'O Bananas!' said they, 'where did you learn that trick, and what have you done to your nose?'

I got a new one from the Crocodile on the banks of the great grey-green, greasy Limpopo River,' said the Elephant's Child. 'I asked him what he had for dinner, and he gave me this to keep.'

'It looks very ugly,' said his hairy uncle, the Baboon.

'It does,' said the Elephant's Child. 'But it's very useful,' and he picked up his hairy uncle, the Baboon, by one hairy leg, and hove him into a hornets' nest.

Then that bad Elephant's Child spanked all his dear families for a long time, till they were very warm and greatly astonished. He pulled out his tall Ostrich aunt's tail-feathers; and he caught his tall uncle, the Giraffe, by the hind-leg, and dragged him through a thorn-bush; and he shouted at his broad aunt, the Hippopotamus, and blew bubbles into her ear when she was sleeping in the water after meals; but he never let any one touch Kolokolo Bird.

At last things grew so exciting that his dear families

went off one by one in a hurry to the banks of the great grey-green, greasy Limpopo River, all set about with fever-trees, to borrow new noses from the Crocodile. When they came back nobody spanked anybody any more; and ever since that day, O Best Beloved, all the Elephants you will ever see, besides all those that you won't, have trunks precisely like the trunks of the 'satiable Elephant's Child.

From *Just So Stories*

Conclusion

I do hope you have enjoyed this book and have perhaps learned something about the animal world. As I mentioned at the beginning of the book, there was a time when horses did a great deal of work for us. But, apart from working for us, animals do give us a tremendous amount of pleasure. For instance, garden birds are beautiful to look at and sing so sweetly. It is true that some of them do a little bit of damage, but a few ruined shoots of green is a small price to pay in return for so much joy and happiness. As you know, the animals of this world have suffered much in the last fifty years. They have been slaughtered for their tusks, for their horns and for their beautiful skins. They have died through our ignorance when we sprayed our farmlands with the most deadly sprays. They are quite helpless against us. They have no guns, no poisons, they do not plan to kill us deliberately, they simply say,

'Look, please leave us alone, watch us if you like but by jingo we'll have to watch you.'

I know that there are a lot of you who would like to work with animals. Some of you will probably get round to doing this but whatever you happen to do in life, keep a place in your heart for the animals. Life would be very empty without them. Good luck!

Johnny Morris

More Beaver Books

We hope you have enjoyed this Beaver Book. Here are some of the other titles:

Animal Quiz A Beaver original. Johnny Morris, universally known and loved for his television programme *Animal Magic*, has created a picture book quiz about all sorts of animals, fish and birds, full of fun and facts for all the family.

The Beaver Book of Pets A Beaver original. A love of animals just isn't enough to help you to look after pets properly. This book tells you how to choose the right pet, how to feed, house and handle it, what it will cost to keep, even how to tell when it's ill. There are detailed chapters on dogs, cats, rabbits, guinea pigs, mice, hamsters, gerbils, birds, horses and ponies, reptiles, guinea pigs, fish, insects and wild animals. Written by Raymond Chaplin and illustrated with black and white photographs and drawings by Tony Morris.

My Favourite Horse Stories Dorian Williams has chosen fifteen of his favourite stories and poems about horses, by authors such as Tolstoy, Shakespeare and Dick Francis; a collection to delight all animal lovers

These and many other Beavers are available from your local bookshop or newsagent, or can be ordered direct from: Hamlyn Paperback Cash Sales, PO Box 11, Falmouth, Cornwall TR10 9EN. Send a cheque or postal order, made payable to The Hamlyn Publishing Group, for the price of the book plus postage at the following rates:

UK: 30p for the first book, 15p for the second book, and 12p for each additional book ordered to a maximum charge of £1.29; BFPO and EIRE: 30p for the first book, 15p for the second book plus 12p per copy for the next 7 books, thereafter 6p per book;

OVERSEAS: 50p for the first book and 15p for each extra book. New Beavers are published every month and if you would like the *Beaver Bulletin*, which gives a complete list of books and prices, including new titles, send a large stamped addressed envelope to:

Beaver Bulletin
Hamlyn Paperbacks
Banda House
Cambridge Grove
Hammersmith
London w6 0LE

203964